RUSSIA AGAINST INDIA

RUSSIA AGAINST INDIA

THE STRUGGLE FOR ASIA

BY

ARCHIBALD R. COLQUHOUN

GYAN

Published by

GYAN

Gyan Publishing House
5, Ansari Road
Daryaganj, New Delhi-110002
Phone: 011-47034999, 9811692060
E-mail: books@gyanbooks.com

Distribution Network
gyanbooks.com
India, USA, Canada, UK, Australia

ISBN: 978-93-6208-206-0 (PB)
First Published, 1900

2nd Impression 2024

Printed at: Gyan Press, Delhi.

RUSSIA AGAINST INDIA
Author: ARCHIBALD R. COLQUHOUN

ASIA

Showing successive advances of Russia

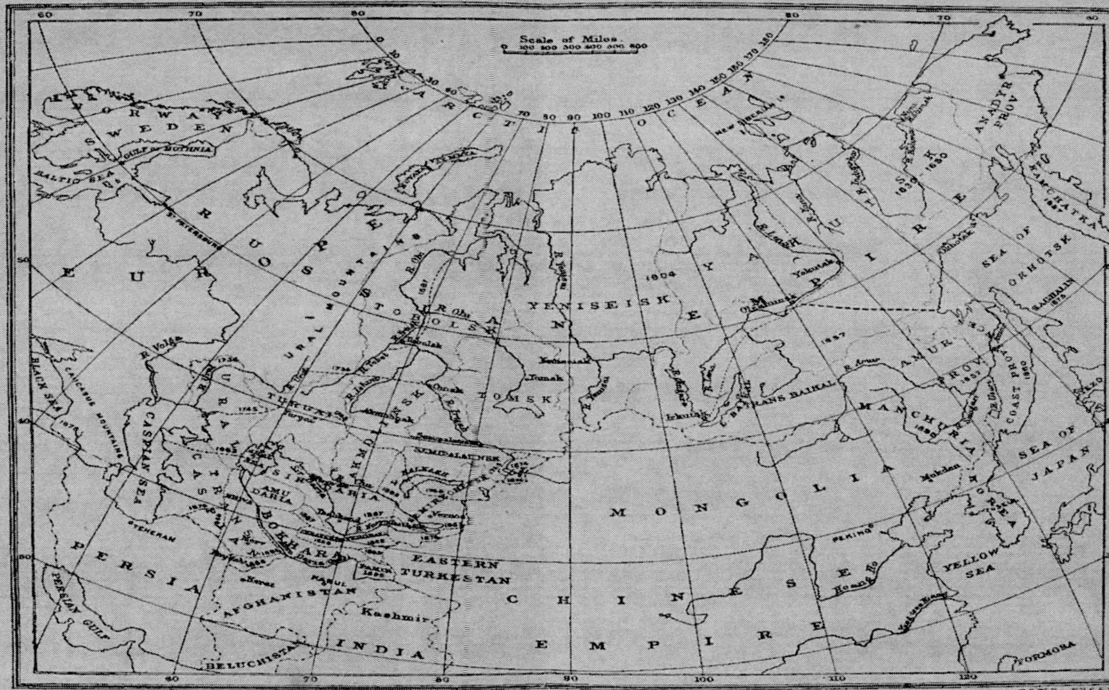

London & New York, Harper & Brothers, 45 Albemarle Street, W.C.

F. S. Weller, F.R.G.S. lith.

RUSSIA AGAINST INDIA

THE STRUGGLE FOR ASIA

BY

ARCHIBALD R. COLQUHOUN

GOLD MEDALLIST, ROYAL GEOGRAPHICAL SOCIETY; FORMERLY DEPUTY COMMISSIONER BURMA; FIRST ADMINISTRATOR OF MASHONALAND, AND SPECIAL CORRESPONDENT OF THE "TIMES" IN THE FAR EAST; AUTHOR OF "ACROSS CHRYSÊ," "CHINA IN TRANSFORMATION," ETC.

WITH SPECIAL MAPS

LONDON AND NEW YORK

HARPER & BROTHERS

45, ALBEMARLE STREET, W.

1901

PREFACE

This little work is intended to bring before the Anglo-Saxon public a question of vital importance. It is not such a complicated and difficult question as is generally supposed, nor is it one that can be shelved for settlement by a future generation. "The man in the street" is nowadays a powerful factor in the facing and solution of political situations, and it is for him that this book has been written, and not for the few experts on the Central Asian question who have already arrived at fixed conclusions. The writer makes no claim to presenting an exhaustive study of the subject, but hopes that his sketch of things, as they are in reality—a sketch from the life, and not from official descriptions—will arouse sufficient interest to induce others to make a study for themselves, and decide in their own minds whether or no it is desirable that the Anglo-Saxon race should be worsted in the "struggle for Asia."

There are many who ridicule the idea of such an impending struggle. Do they base their confidence on the pacific intentions of Russia, or on the impregnability of all other nations with whom she is likely to dispute the possession of Asia? In either case the history of the past throws a significant light on the possibilities of the future. The advance of Russia—"creeping on bit by bit"—is, in this little book, viewed as a whole, and the connection between the transformation of the Far East, especially of China, and the Russian advance towards India through Central Asia, is shown to be intimate.

With British interests in India are closely bound up the interests of the whole Anglo-Saxon race, and indeed of many of the Latin races as well. That these interests are in real jeopardy the writer has endeavoured to make quite plain. It is possible that the whole question may not come to a head during the next few years, but are we not bound to ensure, as far as possible, for those that come after us the prestige our fathers bequeathed us? At the same time, when we take a bird's-eye view of the progress of Russia since the time of Peter the Great, when we look at the maps of Russia then and now—or even the maps of sixty years ago—we may not feel so certain of security even in our own times.

The writer has given the outlines of a policy, at once bold and prudent, which alone would, in his opinion, meet the exigencies of the situation. But no such policy is likely to be initiated unless the People—who govern Governments—instruct themselves, become interested, and demand that measures be taken to safeguard the prestige of the Anglo-Saxon in Asia.

It is a case of educating our masters.

The writer desires to acknowledge his indebtedness, amongst other works, to those of Eugene Schuyler, Hugo Stumm, Thorburn, and the anonymous author of "The March towards India."

A. R. C.

CONTENTS

RUSSIA AGAINST INDIA

THE STRUGGLE FOR ASIA

CHAPTER I

HISTORICAL INTRODUCTION

RUSSIA, at the time of Henry III. in England, some four centuries before the first settlers landed from the *Mayflower* in the United States, was in a state of great disorder, split up into a number of petty principalities, and devastated by Mongol invasions which lasted until the end of the fourteenth century. The Russian princes were mere tax-gatherers, actually forced to pay homage to the Khans of the Golden Horde—a name given to those Mongols who had settled on the banks of the Volga, on account, it is said, of the splendour of their tents and appointments. Obliged to submit their disputes to the decision of the Khan, the Russian princes could not even ascend their thrones without first receiving "Jarlikh," or letters patent, from their Mongol suzerain.

By degrees, however, the Mongol power waned while that of Moscow increased, until, in the reign of Ivan III., who succeeded his father, Vassili the Blind, in 1463, the Muscovites were able to throw off all semblance of obedience to the Horde. In 1478 Ivan refused to pay tribute, trampled on the image of the Khan, and put his envoys to death. The Mongol marched, with a large following, to avenge this insult, and was met by Ivan. The two armies faced each other on either side of the river Oka, but did not come to close quarters, as neither seems to have had the pluck to attack. They contented themselves with an occasional discharge of arrows and more frequent volleys of abuse, and when the freezing of the river made a *rencontre* almost inevitable, both sides were seized with panic, and ran away. The degeneration of the Mongol had, as this incident shows, already made great strides, and from this time the Golden Horde rapidly lost its ascendency. Ere long, indeed, the Grand Prince of Moscow turned the tables on his old suzerain, and both Sarai and Kazan, the headquarters of the two chief Mongol tribes in Russia, were forced to swear allegiance to Moscow; while the Khan of the Crimea, where a third tribe had settled, became a sworn ally of the Grand Prince. About 1499 the Russians made a small raid across the Urals, unimportant in itself, but interesting as their first advance into Asia. Ivan III. had many successes in the battle-field, and, becoming over-lord of a large number of the other States, laid the foundations of, and commenced the work of consolidating, the Russian empire.

The grandson of this prince was Ivan the Terrible, the first to assume the title of "Tsar," who became extremely powerful, and was sought in alliance by ambassadors from Eastern countries. In his time Kazan and Astrakan were annexed, and the Strogonoffs made their colonizing expeditions towards the Urals. The first serious expedition of Russia into Central Asia was undertaken at the end of the sixteenth century by the Kassak (Cossack) tribe, under their celebrated chief, Yermak. These Cossacks were, as their name implies, merely a tribe of outlaws and freebooters, who called themselves "The Good Companions of the Don;" but the Tsar, in order to turn their energies to good purpose, offered them a free pardon if they would assist him against the wild tribes on the other side of the Urals. They accepted the offer, and, crossing the mountains, found their way to the Caspian Sea, where they occupied themselves with piracy and with plundering the Persian colonies. They were, later, also successful in their engagements with the Trans-Ural nomad tribes, whom they completely defeated, taking possession of Sibir, the capital of Kuchum (a lineal descendant of Genghiz Khan), and so giving Russia her first foothold in Asia.* Such was the birth of Russian power in the enormous territory since known to the world as Siberia.

Early in the seventeenth century, some of the Cossacks who had crossed the Urals brought back wonderful tales of riches in the oasis of Khiva, and a troop started thither to explore, taking only such baggage as their horses could carry. At first they were successful, capturing and looting one of the principal towns and annexing a thousand of the youngest and prettiest women for their household requirements; but, encumbered with too much heavy baggage, they were caught and surrounded by

* An account of this is given in "Overland to China."

the Khivans, who shut them off from water. They fought desperately, drinking the blood of the slain to quench their thirst; but though a hundred of them cut their way through and managed to conceal themselves for a time, all eventually perished. Two other campaigns were equally unsuccessful; while the third, which was ostensibly a peaceful mission from Peter the Great to the Khan, ended in the treacherous murder of the Russian envoy and all his men—a Khivan St. Bartholomew's Day.

In the early part of the seventeenth century, relations were established with Bokhara, and it is interesting to note that the Russian ambassadors insisted on being treated with the greatest ceremony. They had "no intention of permitting their nation to be treated with disrespect"—an excellent method in dealing with Asiatics, and one which has been of much service to Russia in her advance into the heart of Asia. China meanwhile viewed the progress of Russia into Asia with distrust, and destroyed the first strongholds which the Russians, taking advantage of a dispute between the Chinese and one of the neighbouring tribes, had built on the Amur. A treaty was concluded later, in 1689, which ousted the Russians altogether from the Amur, and barred their progress towards the Pacific.

The first attempt made by England to trade with Russia was in 1553, when was founded what was known as the British Muscovy Company. Attempts were also made, without much success, to trade with the Khanates of Central Asia through Russia, but the time was not yet ripe; and though an intrepid English sailor, Jenkinson, flew the first British flag on the Caspian Sea and actually reached Bokhara, no regular communication with Central Asia could be established. Owing to their ignorance of geography, Englishmen thought that the only way to reach India—the fabulously wealthy "Kingdom of the Great Mogul"—was through the Tsar's dominions, and it is curious to reflect that the very State to which England looked to afford a means of communication with India is, now that she has built up an Eastern empire for herself, her most dangerous and powerful rival.

Peter the Great, who came to the throne in 1689, adopted the vigorous policy of expansion which has never since ceased to animate his nation. Until early in the eighteenth century he was occupied on the European frontiers of his dominions. His imagination was, however, fired by the wonderful stories which had reached him of the mineral wealth of Siberia, and these were confirmed by an envoy from Khiva, which had some years earlier tendered its submission to the Tsar. Peter, therefore, sent an armed expedition for the double purpose of occupying Khiva and getting some of the gold which, he was assured, was to be found on the shores of the river Oxus. The expedition was a failure, but it resulted in the building of the first fort in the chain, known since as the New Siberian Line, which stretches across the Ishim steppe and was completed in 1752. Peter also established himself firmly on the Caspian Sea, and made efforts to inaugurate a trade-route *viâ* Persia to India. Astrabad, on the Caspian, which was ceded to Russia in 1722, was an important factor in the eyes of the Great Tsar as a base for the advance towards India. "Have you ever been in the Gulf of Astrabad?" he exclaimed to an officer at Derbent. "You must know, then, that those mountains"—pointing to the heights on the shores of the Caspian—"extend to Astrabad; and from there to Balkh and Badakshan with pack-camels is only a twelve days' journey, and on that road to India no one can interfere with us."

Peter died in 1725, and after his death Russian affairs in Asia were for some time less successfully conducted. The document known as the "Will of Peter the Great" was almost certainly apocryphal, and not improbably written at the instigation of Napoleon I. It sets forth a policy, however, virtually amounting to the conquest of Asia and, through Asia, of the world.* It expresses, in fact, the true aspirations of the Russian nation, and Russian diplomatists have, since the time of Peter the Great, steadily pursued a course in keeping with the principles set forth in this document. Towards the end of the eighteenth century, in the reign of the Empress Catherine II., a scheme was contemplated, the first of its kind, for invading India through the Khanates of Central Asia—a scheme which was, however, never carried into effect.

For the rest of the century Russia was occupied with her European conquests. The annexation of the Crimea in 1775 was marked by a merciless slaughter of 30,000 Tartars of either sex and every age. Georgia, which

* See Appendix.

had been a shuttlecock between Persia and Russia for some time, became the vassal of the latter in 1800. A year later the Emperor Paul, infatuated with Napoleon, agreed to a project for the joint invasion of India by France and Russia. The orders had already been given to the commander, and an army of Cossacks had started, when the death of the Tsar put an end to the scheme. His successor, Alexander I., did not pursue the project, but he continued the struggle to extend his dominions into Central Asia, and a long conflict with Persia ensued, in which the fate of Georgia and other Caucasian provinces was disputed without any decided advantage to either side.

Napoleon, having defeated Austria and Russia at Austerlitz in 1805, tried to undermine the interests of Russia in Asia by seeking an alliance with Persia; but a treaty had already been concluded with Britain, and the policy of the Shah was to keep both French and Russians at bay, looking to Great Britain for aid, in return for which he was to prevent the Afghans from invading India. In 1807, however, finding that Great Britain would not afford him the aid he wanted, the Shah concluded a treaty with

Napoleon; and, when the Peace of Tilsit put an end to the war between France and Russia, Alexander and Napoleon concocted another scheme for the invasion of India, in which they counted upon Persia as an ally. But the French had overreached themselves, and the British envoy, Sir Harford Jones, succeeded in persuading the Shah that the true enemy of Persia must always be Russia, and her friends those who are against that Power. As the Tsar had just declared war with France, and as Persia had, despite promises, reaped no advantages from her French alliance, this diplomacy was successful, and an Anglo-Persian treaty was again concluded. Sir Harford Jones appears to have been "the first British statesman to realize that the greatest external danger which threatened British India was to be found, not in French intrigues at Teheran, nor in the possibility of invasion by Afghan hordes, but in the steady and insidious encroachments of Russia beyond her European frontiers." The close of the year 1814 found Persia, though some of her fairest provinces had been ceded to Russia, at peace with that nation and in alliance with Great Britain, the latter Power undertaking to defend her in a war with any European nation, unless she herself were the aggressor. Russia, however, by her threatening attitude on the Persian frontier, which had not been accurately defined, provoked the Persians to declare war, and, when applied to for help, the British Government elected to abide by the letter of the treaty rather than risk a war with a European nation. In the subsequent struggle Persia lost still more provinces to Russia. When peace was concluded, Russia turned her attention to Turkey, and conducted a successful campaign which enabled her to round off her possessions south of the Caucasus. She then began to undermine British influence in the court of Teheran, and to stir up Persia to make attacks on Afghanistan. Mr. McNeill, the British envoy and afterwards ambassador, was not able to prevent a campaign, although he did everything in his power. Great Britain, being bound by the terms of the former treaty, was unable to interfere, and the English, who had formerly urged the Persians to attack Afghanistan (for the purpose of shielding India from an Afghan invasion), now had the mortification of seeing a Persian army (largely drilled by British officers) repeat that invasion, not in defence of British interests, but to further the designs of Russia upon the British Empire in India. The first British-Afghan war took place in 1839, resulting in the occupation of the chief cities by British troops.

Russia now began a policy of slow but systematic advance in Central Asia. In the winter of 1839 an expedition, starting from Orenburg, was led by General Perovski, ostensibly to obtain the release of Russian prisoners in Khiva, and to redress the injuries inflicted by the wild tribes on the borders of Russia; in reality, the object was to obtain paramount influence over Afghanistan, and to oust the British. That winter, however, proved to be one of almost unprecedented rigour in Central Asia, and after horrible sufferings, entailed by the effort to march in blinding storms with snow almost waist high, the troops returned to Orenburg, leaving more than a thousand dead, and bringing 609 sick to be lodged in hospital. This expedition, nevertheless, convinced the Khivans that Russia was in earnest, and to avert another campaign, the Khan made overtures, and sent back many prisoners, but it was not till 1842 that a treaty was concluded.

The Khanate of Khiva is a long, narrow oasis, including both banks of the Amu Daria, and extending from the frontier of Bokhara to the southern shore of the Sea of Aral. The city of Khiva is the exact centre of the Khanate. A girdle of absolute desert, in area exceeding the territories of Germany, France, and Italy together, with a radius of over fifty miles, encircles Khiva on every side, in many places attaining a width of from fifty-five to sixty miles. This girdle was surrounded from the south-west round to the north-east by Russian territory, Russian forts, and Russian troops. The south and south-east were bordered by Persia, Afghanistan, and Bokhara, and could only be of importance if these states abandoned their neutrality.

Khiva was one of the most sacred cities of Central Asia, and, according to an old saying, would remain secure from foreign aggression—interpreted as Russian—until the waters of the Amu Daria, returning to the old bed which they had deserted, should once more wash against the walls of Kane Urgench (the old capital, which lies north of Khiva). In 1839 the river is said to have risen to such an extent that its waters reached the ancient city, and the inhabitants, whose superstition is notorious, felt the hour for Russia had come.

From the time of her first steps in expansion, Russia invariably marked her line of advance with forts, which gradually extended further south and east. These were occupied by Cossacks, who were able to combine agricultural with military pursuits, and thus to a certain extent mitigate the grave difficulties of provisioning. These Cossacks were able to hold the forts against overwhelming odds.

The disasters which befell the British in Afghanistan during the years 1841–42 brought about a marked difference in the attitude of Russia towards the Khanates, and the misfortunes of the British quite dwarfed those of Perovski, which had created so powerful an impression throughout Russia. These disasters began with the attempt of Dost Mohammed to regain his throne, from which Britain had deposed him. This attempt was unsuccessful, but the people were discontented, and the Suddozai Shah, the British nominee, was unpopular. The disaffection grew, unchecked by any prompt action on the part of the British, until it culminated in the murder at Kabul of Sir Alexander Burnes and the British envoy, Sir William Macnaghten. Matters then went rapidly from bad to worse, and ended disastrously in the retreat of General Elphinstone, with an army of 16,000, of which only one man, Dr. Bryden, was ever destined to reach Jalalabad alive. The English position in Afghanistan seemed almost hopeless, and, to crown all, at Bokhara two British envoys, Stoddart and Conolly, who had been sent on special missions, were cruelly put to death by the Amir, who thought he had nothing to fear from the countrymen of a nation which had just sustained so terrible a defeat. The Russian agent, Buteneff, on the contrary, who was accompanied by a small staff of miners and topographers, was well received at first, and made valuable notes and extensive surveys. Buteneff, however, could not effect any agreement with the Amir, and finally left without the usual official ceremony, feeling by no means certain that he might not share the fate of the unfortunate Englishmen who had lost their lives, if he stayed longer with the treacherous Amir.

While England was preparing to retrieve the disgrace of Kabul, Russia took an opportunity offered her by Persia, who appealed for aid to check the piracy of the Turkomans on the Caspian Sea. By the treaty of Turkomanchi,

Persia had forfeited the right to keep war-vessels on this sea, but Russia was hampered by no such restriction. She sent ships from the naval station on the island of Sari, and took possession of Ashurada (at the mouth of the Gulf of Astrabad), which she proceeded to fortify. Despite the protests of Persia, who appealed to England for aid, this place was held, and has ever since remained the property of the Tsar. This, one of Russia's bloodless conquests, acquired simply by a cool, high-handed, and unscrupulous policy, affords her one of the most valuable strategical positions in Central Asia.

The Kirghiz, who were nominally the vassals of Russia, now gave her an excellent pretext for pushing the line of forts further south. They had never abandoned their predatory habits, and frequently attacked the caravans which passed across their steppes. At the beginning of the century Russia adopted more stringent measures, and large bodies of Cossacks were sent to subdue them. During the first half of the century the line of forts had been thrown out till it almost enclosed a large portion of the Kirghiz steppe, but a considerable gap was left between Fort Raim, on the Aral Sea, and Kopal. To connect these was now the aim of the Russian Government, and, as a preliminary, an expedition was sent up the Syr Daria with the object of founding a fort there. The Khokandians viewed these advances with much uneasiness, and resisted to the best of their power. Ak-Mechet, the important fortress of Khokand, was twice besieged—in 1852, and again in the following year—and finally captured. Several attempts were made to regain it, and great numbers of Khokandians killed, but it remained in the hands of the Russians. Almost simultaneously an advance was made in the east, from Kopal, and the excuse offered was that the Kirghiz Kazaks must be defended from their wild kinsmen, the Kara Kirghiz, who inhabited the mountainous districts. Either the Kirghiz must themselves be brought to order, or they must be protected; in either case the paternal Government must send a large body of troops, and the ascendency of the White Tsar thoroughly established. Acting on Peter the Great's saying, "The Kirghiz are a roaming and fickle people, but their country is the key and gate to all the lands of Central Asia," the Russians have always used them as a means to the great end they have in view. As, however, the whole country of the Kirghiz is now under Russian rule, excuses are no longer needed.

In 1854 a scheme for the invasion of India was prepared by General Duhamel, and presented to the Tsar, to whom it was pointed out that there were five routes by which Russia might proceed, and that if the friendship of Afghanistan in particular could be gained, the path to victory would be easy. This invasion would further effect the object of withdrawing the whole attention of Great Britain from the war just begun in the Crimea. The victories of the allied armies of England and France prevented the realization of this scheme; and though suggestions were made at the time that this would be a good occasion for the British to emulate the policy of Russia herself, by advancing into Central Asia and driving her back, yet nothing of the sort was attempted.

A few years later, in 1857, two embassies came to St. Petersburg from Khiva and Bokhara, both asking for the friendship of the Tsar. Count Ignatieff was accordingly entrusted with a mission to Bokhara, with directions to proceed thither by way of Khiva, in order to conclude a treaty with the Khan and obtain permission to navigate the Amu Daria and examine the ancient river-bed of the Oxus. Unsuccessful in Khiva, he was well received in Bokhara. At the same time three different parties were engaged in exploring respectively the country between the Urals and the Caspian, that beyond Lake Balkash and the Thian Shan range, and Kashgaria. Valuable information regarding Eastern Turkestan was obtained, and a large portion of the country surrounding the Caspian was mapped out. An important mission under Khanikoff explored Khorassan, starting in 1858, and, travelling from Astrabad to Herat, returned to Teheran. At Herat Khanikoff set afoot intrigues against England, then in the throes of the Indian Mutiny, but his attempt at diplomacy was not successful.

So far, the Russians had not yet completed the connection of their chain of forts; but in 1859 the Khokandian stronghold of Julek, on the Syr Daria, was captured, and in 1861 rebuilt under the name of Fort Perovski. The Khokandians mustered a large army, but were utterly routed; and their defeat was followed in 1864 by the loss of Hazret-i-Turkestan. Here the two Russian columns joined hands, and were combined under Tchernaieff. Chimkent, the most advanced Khokandian fortress, still remained intact, and was garrisoned with 10,000 men. It was asserted that so large an armed body could not be allowed to exist in such close proximity to the Russian frontier, and accordingly, in October, 1864, Chimkent was seized by means of a daring *coup*. This laid the road open to Tashkent, the capital, an opportunity of which Tchernaieff was not slow to avail himself. After a severe struggle, Tashkent surrendered in June, 1865, and the fate of Khokand was finally sealed. These campaigns did not seem to excite much apprehension in Great Britain, and Lord Lawrence, then Viceroy of India, was inculcating the doctrine that "Russia might prove a safer neighbour than the wild tribes of Central Asia." Nevertheless, the Russian Chancellor, Prince Gortchakoff, felt it necessary to explain the position and intentions of his country to the world at large, and accordingly issued the now famous circular of November 21, 1864, which explained the Asiatic policy of Russia, and utterly denied her intention of acquiring any further dependencies in Central Asia.*

* See Appendix.

Seid Mosaffer, the Amir of Bokhara in 1865, was a successor of Tamerlane, and regarded himself as the suzerain of all the Khanates and the defender of the Mohammedan faith. He sought to make capital out of the internal dissensions of Khokand, took several of the principal cities, and established a new Khan. General Tchernaieff sent an embassy to him under Colonel von Struve, which, though well received, was not permitted to depart, but was kept in confinement for six months—until, indeed, serious reverses to the arms of Bokhara had somewhat frightened the Amir. He then addressed a despatch to General Romanovski, expressing the sincere wish "to live at peace with Russia;" but, at the same time, he was actively engaged in preparations for another campaign, which assumed large proportions, being proclaimed by the fanatical mollahs as a sacred war of vengeance. This war was terminated by the siege of Samarkand, which was taken by Russia and held despite the most determined assaults. The defenders retired to the citadel, the town having been betrayed by some of the native inhabitants, and had hardly time to close the gates; here they managed to hold out—although provisions and ammunition ran short and 200 men were killed—until relieved by the rest of the army. Despite the assurances of the Russian ambassador in England that the Tsar did not intend to retain this city, it was never again ceded to the Amir. Seid Mosaffer was so disheartened by his reverses that he wished to abdicate and go on a pilgrimage to Mecca, but it was important that Bokhara should have a ruler who fully realized the power of Russia. It was also considered more politic to have a responsible satrap to rule over the Tsar's southern protectorate than to waste men and money on a complete military occupation. The Amir, therefore, was politely requested to resume his throne, and, nominally independent, became the obedient vassal of Russia.

The subjugation of Bokhara was followed by the Steppe Commission, which published an ukase in 1867 announcing the formation of the province of Turkestan, to include the whole of the recently acquired territories, with headquarters at Tashkent, and ruled by a Governor-General appointed at St. Petersburg.

The British Government now became alarmed at the advance of Russia, and the idea of a "neutral zone" between Russia and India, with a view to obviating further difficulties, was suggested. Finally, after much dispute as to the limitary line, the Agreement of 1873 was concluded, and Russia undertook not to interfere with Afghanistan. The north-eastern and north-western frontiers were, however, very ambiguously described—a fact utilized by Russia, who, after the occupation of Merv, seized a large slice of territory in the neighbourhood.

The province of Prilinsk, formerly Kuldja, was annexed in 1868, Russia having become alarmed lest it should fall into the hands of Yakoob Beg, the enterprising ruler of Kashgar. Originally occupied by Mongolian tribes, Kuldja had been colonized by the Chinese, to whom it virtually belonged until annexed by Russia, who promised to restore it as soon as the Emperor of China could send a sufficient force to occupy it.

A commercial treaty had been signed in 1874 between Great Britain and Kashgaria, but the invasion by China of the Eastern frontier, and the death of Yakoob Beg, altered the position of affairs. China was entirely successful, and, having established herself firmly in Eastern Turkestan, was in a position to comply with the conditions on which Russia had promised to give back Kuldja, and promptly demanded its rendition. After much negotiation, the demand was partially acceded to, but the complete evacuation did not take place till 1883.

The occupation of Krasnovodsk on the Caspian Sea, in 1869, gave Russia a position from which she could exercise a threatening influence on the borders of the Herat province, and serious apprehensions were also felt at Khiva. The Russian Government, however, announced that Krasnovodsk was merely to be used as a factory, and not for strategical purposes. The entire eastern coast of the Caspian Sea is, with a few exceptions, destitute of vegetation, while the interior, as far as the oasis of Khiva, has no settled inhabitants. Tribes of Kirghiz and Turkomans visit it periodically, but the district barely affords sufficient nourishment even for their hardy horses and camels. The country between the Amu and Syr Daria is equally barren, and the few nomads settled on the Russian frontier, in the Orenburg Government, are sometimes, like birds of passage, seized with the old wandering instinct, and "trek" to the plains of Western Siberia, so rich in grass, or to the Southern Ural steppes, or to the Ust Urt, which lies between the Caspian and the Sea of Aral.

Khiva was the door of all commercial routes to the centre of Asia, but the lesson learnt from previous diplomacy and campaigns was that this door would never open to peaceful negotiations, but only to force. It was felt that the base for successful operations against Khiva was the Caspian Sea, and a line of forts was planned on the east coast. Krasnovodsk was to become a considerable port, and energetic measures were adopted towards the neighbouring Yomud and Tekké tribes. Warfare with these people was carried on under difficulties, for they deserted their forts at the approach of the enemy and carried off all their goods and chattels. The future hero of Plevna, then Colonel Skobeleff, accompanied by three Cossacks, disguised as Usbek merchants, succeeded in penetrating right into the cultivated parts of the oasis of Khiva; and, passing safely through the hostile nomads who kept their flocks there, returned to Tiflis without misadventure, and added much to the scanty knowledge hitherto possessed of these regions.

The following year an expedition under

Markasoff reached the same spot on the Amu Daria, and supplied valuable information as to the country through which they had passed. Thanks to Skobeleff, they were able to arrange their halts so as to strike the principal wells, which are sometimes very bitter, but can be used for cooking purposes. The Khivan desert, consisting of hot, dry, and yielding sand, was trying to march through, but they had the advantage of a cool wind. From the spot mentioned, Sari Kamish, on the dried-up watercourse of the river Oxus, Markasoff made a reconnaissance, and, coming across some fresh-water pools in the ancient river-bed, was able to verify Skobeleff's visit there in a curious way. Close to one of the wells he picked up a silver teaspoon with that officer's initials, which had been dropped there a year before. On the return march towards Krasnovodsk, Markasoff gradually re-collected his forces, which he had disposed in small forts along his route. All the wells of the Khivan desert have names, many relating to some event in their history. One at which Markasoff halted was called Topiatan, or "the well to which cannon has been dragged," tradition relating that a Khivan chief once on a time dragged a gun to this very spot, with the purpose of resisting the Russians. No trace, however, of this murderous Asiatic weapon now remains. During the retreat, Markasoff had a miraculous escape at one of the halting-places, for the camp was besieged on all sides, and the Turkomans made a desperate attempt to kill him, even bursting into his tent and killing his guards. Luckily for himself, the general was away visiting the outposts, and the Turkomans had to retire without accomplishing their object.

In 1872–73 Markasoff conducted a campaign against the Tekkés, with Khiva as an ultimate goal. The Tekkés were a martial race, and had built a number of small mud fortresses, very primitive works indeed, which were, however, deemed impregnable by the neighbouring tribes. They were simply squares composed of mud walls, without fortifications, the *kibitkas*, or tents, being ranged both inside and around the fortress. Though essentially nomad in character and habits, the Tekkés are fond of agriculture, and notwithstanding that the country is badly watered, they grow vegetables, grain, and cotton in the neighbourhood of their dwellings. The Tekkés adopted a very simple plan of warfare on the approach of Markasoff—they burnt their *kibitkas* and fled. Eventually, however, they came to close quarters and were defeated at Dshmala, after which they sent an embassy to Markasoff to assure him of their friendship, and to ask for the release of the prisoners in the hands of the Russians. They made the original excuse for their hostile attitude that they had supposed Russian soldiers to be no better than Persians. Markasoff wishing, according to the Russian account, to propitiate them "by kindness," gave up the prisoners; but as these would have been a hindrance to him on the march, and would have consumed water, which was scarce, there would seem to have been a certain motive of policy in his action. Markasoff asked for a tribute of 300 camels, which, by the way, he never succeeded in getting. His column, although useful as affording valuable opportunities for surveying the country, was not destined to reach Khiva. The Turkomans attacked him persistently, and he thought it wiser to retire. The Russian Government, however, by no means abandoned the idea, and an elaborate campaign was arranged by which five columns converged from different points upon Khiva. All but that under the command of Markasoff reached their destination; and in June, 1873, Khiva capitulated to General Kauffmann, and the Khan, although permitted to retain his throne, became the mere puppet of Russia. The Tekké tribes continued to give considerable trouble, and another unsuccessful expedition was conducted against them in 1879; but it was not until 1881 that the Russian troops under Skobeleff were able to entirely subdue them.

CHAPTER II

HISTORICAL INTRODUCTION—*continued*

It may be said with truth that every kingdom, principality, or tribe to which Russia has extended "protection," has eventually been appropriated into the Muscovite Empire. In Europe she has gradually acquired Finland, Livonia, Lithuania, a large portion of Poland, Bessarabia, and other territories. Finding, however, that further extension in Europe is impracticable, unless, indeed, at immense sacrifice of life and money, she has for many years turned her attention to the more open field of Central Asia, where, carrying out a policy similar to that pursued in Europe, she has by degrees pushed her way through tribe after tribe, protecting and annexing as she went, until, at the present moment, she has practically arrived at the gates of Afghanistan. This, of course, is not the proposed end of her march. During this progress of hers, the Kalmuck and Kirghiz tribes had, amongst others, to be dealt with; and it is significant that the former, in 1771, unable to longer endure the Russian oppression, migrated to Chinese territory to the number of half a million, having to fight their way thither through hostile tribes. The Kirghiz, however, whose land, according to Peter the Great, is "the key and gate to all the countries of Asia," were not so fortunate in maintaining their independence, for they gradually fell before the inevitable wave of Russian advance; and although many of them do not even now acknowledge allegiance to the conqueror, the majority are both nominally and practically vassals of the Tsar, their patriarchal system having been gradually superseded by that of circuits and volosts, and their very wanderings being carefully regulated by the governor of their province.

The race is undoubtedly of great antiquity. Their early government was founded on the patriarchal system, their chiefs being known as Khans. Tradition says that one of these early Khans divided his kingdom into three parts for his sons, thus founding the three Hordes—the Great, Middle, and Lesser. The second of these, living on the western frontier of China, and consequently at a great distance from Russia, preserved their independence until as late as 1847. The Lesser Horde, occupying the country contiguous to the possessions of Russia in the southern Ural, and the Great Horde, living mostly north and east of the Sea of Aral, being torn by internal dissensions and harried by neighbouring tribes, offered their allegiance to Russia in 1730, but at that time it was not accepted. Shortly afterwards, however, the Russian Empress consented to become suzerain and protectress of the Kirghiz, a step which has since led to the acquisition of much territory on the part of Russia, although no inconsiderable amount of money, not to speak of human life, has been sacrificed in the process.

At first Russia's policy in Central Asia was to control her subjects by playing off one tribe against another, thus keeping them well occupied. As it was found, however, that the predatory habits of the Kirghiz (by no means renounced when they took the oath of allegiance to the White Tsar) greatly interfered with the caravan trade which Russia was anxious to develop; and that they made raids on Russian colonists on the frontier line and along the shores of the

Caspian, carrying off many of the settlers and selling them as slaves, expeditions were frequently sent to bring them to order. The Kirghiz resisted stoutly, and as late as 1843, rallying round their popular Khan Kenissar, the "Kirghiz Schamyl," met with a certain amount of success, and were hopeful of achieving their independence. With the death of Kenissar in 1846, however, this hope was destroyed, and, as previously stated, their final subjection to the Muscovite was merely a matter of time. A kibitka tax of 36,000 roubles is now levied on the Kirghiz of the Caucasian province.

At a time when the Tsar's troops were making steady progress in Central Asia among these Kirghiz and other tribes, there arose, in the Christian provinces of the Turkish Empire, disturbances which eventually led to the Russo-Turkish war. The enmity between Christians and Moslems had led to fearful massacres in Bulgaria; Bosnia, Herzegovina, and Montenegro were in revolt; and in the summer of 1876 Servia declared war against the Turks. When the latter, however, were on the point of taking Belgrade, Russia interfered, and demanded that an armistice of six weeks should be agreed to.

Negotiations were carried on for a considerable time, a conference of the Powers being held at Constantinople early in 1877; but as no satisfactory result was arrived at, the Tsar, in April of that year, having invoked the Supreme blessing, ordered his troops to cross the Turkish frontier, declaring that his "desire to ameliorate and assure the lot of the oppressed Christian population of Turkey" left him no alternative. And so it came about that, whilst thus engaged, Russia's attention was for a brief period partially diverted from her designs on the various approaches to the Indian Empire. The Russo-Turkish campaign was carried on, not only in Europe, but also in Turkey's Asiatic provinces, Armenia being invaded by Russian troops. In the spring of 1878 Russia had obtained possession of all the Armenian fortresses, and, with an army encamped near the Golden Horn found Constantinople at her mercy. The occupation of the city, at that time apparently imminent, did not, however, take place, for at this point a British fleet arrived on the scene, anchoring in the Bosphorus. Shortly after this the Russians effected an occupation of the village of San Stefano, and eventually the war was brought to a close (March 3, 1878) by the Treaty of San Stefano, after some delay on the part of the Turks in agreeing to the proposed terms.

During the war Russia had been ill-pleased to find that England had despatched Indian troops into Europe, and when the British Government insisted that the terms of the Treaty of San Stefano should be laid before a congress of the European Powers, relations between the two countries became so strained that both nations began to prepare for war. In order that Britain's action in Europe should be weakened as much as possible, by forcing her to confine her attention to the defence of her Eastern empire, a demonstration against India was decided upon. Under Skobeleff's scheme for the invasion of that country through Afghanistan, the first step was to be an alliance with Shere Ali (who had hitherto been an ally of Britain), and increased efforts were made to bring to a successful issue the negotiations which emissaries of the Tsar had for some years been carrying on with the Amir. That potentate was informed that if he refused to become the tool of Russia, another claimant to his throne would be brought forward and backed by Russian influence. Under this pressure the Amir yielded, rejecting with insolence the overtures of the British, who wished to send a mission to Kabul. Stolietoff's mission to that city in 1878 ended in the conclusion of an alliance having for its object a joint attack by Russia and Afghanistan on India; an alliance which was the result of seven years' careful intriguing carried on by Kauffmann's agents at the Afghan capital. Simultaneously, an emissary was secretly despatched to India to sow the seeds of rebellion; but on reaching Peshawur he was arrested, and, despite the outcry at interference with a "private traveller," was quietly sent down country and deported to Russia. Meanwhile, however, the Berlin Congress had met, and had rendered any advance of Russia on India an impossibility for the time being. Shere Ali found himself between two stools. The English were demanding reparation, and an army was marching towards Kabul, while the Russians refused, perforce, all aid, and would not even mediate. The course of action pursued by Russia at this time will long be remembered as treacherous, not only towards the Amir, but also Great Britain; for Stolietoff stayed at

Kabul five months after the Treaty of Berlin was concluded, and acted as adviser to Shere Ali till such time as the unfortunate Amir was compelled to fly to the north, accompanying the Russian mission, and leaving his son, Yakoob Khan, as regent. The British established their ascendency over Afghanistan, concluded the Treaty of Gandamak, left a British resident at Kabul, and, having established their supremacy, withdrew their troops. By this treaty certain valleys were assigned to the British Government, which obtained complete control over the Khyber and Michni passes; while, in return for support against foreign aggression and an annual subsidy of six lakhs of rupees, the new Amir bound himself to conduct his relations with other states in accordance with the advice of the Indian Government. With regard to the conduct of Russia in sending Stolietoff to Kabul, it must be remembered that in 1869, and again in 1873, she had given the most solemn assurances, which were repeated from time to time, that Afghanistan should not be tampered with, and that Russian agents should not visit Kabul. In spite of this, however, Russian officers and Cossacks, as has been said, remained at Kabul for five months after the Treaty of Berlin was signed, and this although M. de Giers, in July, 1878, gave assurance to the British ambassador at St. Petersburg that "no mission had been, or was intended to be, sent to Kabul, either by the Imperial Government or by General Kauffmann." A month later, when the state of affairs could no longer be concealed (as accounts of the progress of the mission were actually appearing in the Russian press), de Giers informed the British *chargé d'affaires* that "everything had been stopped; the political as well as the military precautions which we thought ourselves justified in taking against you—everything has been stopped." Nevertheless, four months later, in a conversation with the British Prime Minister, Count Schouvaloff casually observed that, although the Russian envoy who had been sent to Afghanistan had been recalled, the Russian mission still remained at Kabul. Nothing could better illustrate the fine distinctions which characterize the general policy of Russia in Central Asia, where, to quote Prince Dolgoroukoff, "slavish subjection and arbitrary force reign from top to bottom, and throughout there is developed in formidable proportions the official lie—the lie erected into a political institution." One more significant incident. When the Treaty of Berlin rendered imperative the retirement of the troops which were gathered to invade India, Grodekoff, the chief of the staff, left Samarkand, with General Kauffmann's permission, and, wearing his uniform, rode through Northern Afghanistan to Herat, an escort of Afghan troopers being furnished as soon as he had crossed the Russo-Afghan frontier. At Herat he was accorded a warm reception, and after staying there three days and making a thorough survey of the city and its fortifications, continued his journey to Meshed, and thence to Astrabad. On returning to Russia he was cordially received by the Tsar, knighted, and appointed Governor of the Syr Daria district, from which he has since been moved to still higher command.

Under all the circumstances it is apparent that Russia's action in Central Asia at that time is not to be viewed solely in the light of precautionary measures, in case of hostilities with Great Britain. In reality, the Tsar's Government saw a chance to make another step forward in the direction of India, and they did not neglect the opportunity.

Another means by which Russia had long sought to approach nearer to her goal was by getting a footing in the Akhal country, and she never rested till, having conquered the Turkomans of Akhal and Merv, she was able to establish garrisons close to Herat, the "Key of India"—the English, in their horror of a great war, permitting her to thus take possession of a part of Afghanistan, and to occupy advantageous positions in the country. In 1877 an expedition under Lomakin had been sent against the Akhal Tekkés, but met with disastrous failure, which, coming just at the time when Russia had sustained her reverse at Plevna, considerably reduced her prestige in Central Asia. In the following year Lomakin undertook a second expedition, which, however, was even less successful than the first; but the Russians were not to be beaten, and they set about retrieving their position. Still another campaign was organized, General Lazareff being appointed to the command; but disaster continued to attend the Russian arms, for Lazareff, falling a victim to the poisonous air and the impure water supply characteristic of the Caspian shores, died just as the troops were entering the

Akhal territory. After his death, Lomakin was again placed in command; but at Denghil Tepé, where the Tekkés made a resolute stand, he lost his final chance of retrieving his former failures, and after a wanton massacre, in which he spared neither women nor children, was himself driven back, and his troops overwhelmed by the desperate Tekkés. Alikhanoff, an eye-witness of what took place, says, "The whole course of the battle, . . . from beginning to end, was in defiance of the commonest elementary rules of the art of war." At this last reverse, Russian prestige, of course, sank to the lowest ebb, and for the time being the campaign against the Tekkés was abandoned.

Meanwhile, English supremacy had apparently been firmly re-established in Afghanistan by the Treaty of Gandamak, and it was supposed that Yakoob Khan would be strong enough to hold his own against the various factions in the country. The British congratulated themselves on the turn which affairs had taken, while Russia looked on in mortification and alarm at the advantages which had accrued to her rival. At this juncture, however, an event occurred which rendered necessary a second British campaign against Afghanistan. A few days prior to Lomakin's defeat at Denghil Tepé, news arrived of the treacherous murder of Sir Louis Cavagnari, who had just been appointed British resident at Kabul, and who, with his officers, was set upon by certain of the fanatical inhabitants of that city (September, 1879). The British took up arms to avenge his murder and to vindicate their supremacy. Yakoob Khan was deposed, and Abdul Rahman Khan was made Amir in his place; but although the campaign was entirely successful, the English Government, under Mr. Gladstone, did not think it advisable to retain the country which had been won at so much cost; and accordingly, in 1881, Afghanistan was entirely evacuated, it being maintained that a Russian invasion of India was a very remote contingency, and that "the probability of our having to struggle for Herat, or to defend India from Kandahar, is so remote that its possibility is hardly worth considering."

In the same year in which Afghanistan was thus evacuated, Skobeleff triumphed over the Tekkés; and with the fall of Denghil Tepé, the power of the Akhal Turkomans was entirely broken. Skobeleff estimated the total loss of the Turkomans during this last siege to be about 20,000, or half the defenders of the town.

The occupation of Merv seemed likely to be the next item on the Russian programme; but this, M. de Giers assured Lord Dufferin, was far from being the case. "Not only do we not want to go there, but happily there is nothing that can require us to go there."

In response to anxious inquiries on the part of Great Britain, the Russo-Persian frontier was at last definitely fixed, in 1881, by the Convention of Teheran; but the most important part of the frontier-line, that between Merv and Herat, was not included in the arrangement. During the next few years Russia resorted to her favourite expedient, and sent agents, under the guise of scientific and trading explorers, who made a careful reconnaissance of the oasis of Merv, and the routes thither. The occupation and annexation of the town, early in 1884, was well timed, taking place at a moment when Great Britain was wholly occupied with affairs in the Soudan. It was practically accomplished by the intimidation of the inhabitants, who, being overawed by the Russian troops who had been gradually introduced into their country, swore allegiance, through their chiefs, to the White Tsar. The news was thereupon conveyed to England, his Imperial Majesty intimating that he had decided to accept the allegiance, and had sent an officer to administer the region. The possession of the Merv oasis, it may be observed, is of the utmost advantage to Russia, both strategically and commercially. Before the annexation of Merv, the Russian armies of the Trans-Caspian and of Turkestan were separated by a large tract of hostile country, and, as can readily be seen, in the event of a war with England, such an arrangement would have been far from conducive to the success of the Russian arms. Once Merv was taken, however, the position of affairs was entirely altered, for free and direct communication was thus obtained from the Caspian Sea to the borders of China, whilst, at the same time, a shorter route by way of Askabad, Merv, and Charjui was provided for the sending of reinforcements to the Turkestan army. The saving of time immediately effected by making use of this route could be estimated in weeks, and when the railway had been carried through Merv and Charjui to Samarkand might be reckoned in months. The commercial gain to Russia consequent on the acquisition of Merv is no less important than the strategical, for new markets have been opened up for the interchange of both European and Asiatic commodities, and by this means a great impetus has been given to the Central Asian cotton trade.

But, of course, whatever immediate advantages might accrue to Russia, there is little room to doubt that her ulterior object in acquiring the place was to advance yet another step on her carefully planned path towards India, and it was not long before she found fresh opportunity for her enterprise. Her troops had now been introduced to a district whose frontiers towards Afghanistan were but imperfectly defined, and where, in consequence, the possibilities were illimitable. Further developments were rapid.

Immediately after the annexation of Merv, a new map was prepared by Russia, in which she took advantage of a certain vagueness of definition as to desert land (so called in the Anglo-Russian agreement of 1873, by which the frontier had till this time been delimitated) to extend her boundaries. In answer to repeated inquiries on the part of Great Britain, it was arranged that a Boundary Commission should meet at Sarakhs in October of 1884. Various expedients were, however, resorted to by Russia in order to gain time; and meanwhile she occupied numerous points of vantage. In January, 1885, she herself proposed a frontier line which would be much to her own advantage, and which practically meant that Britain should agree, without any inquiry, to a Russian appropriation of Pandjeh and neighbouring districts, hitherto considered as parts of Afghanistan. This was, of course, rejected by the British Government, who, however, made a counter-proposal, in which considerable concessions were made to Russia. Their proposition did not meet with the approval of the Russians, who now no longer endeavoured to conceal the fact that their intention was to occupy all the important points on the way to Herat. The British Government thereupon made strong representations on the subject, and demanded that Russian troops should be withdrawn from certain outlying positions which they already held, and that no further advance should be made. The Russians refused to evacuate any position already in their possession, but agreed to the second half of the demand. The promise was, as usual, not carried out, and attempts were made at various points to provoke the Afghans to hostilities. The despatch received at Kabul from the British Government hereupon gave distinct instructions on the subject: "Her Majesty's Government cannot advise the Afghans to attack the Russian troops in order to dislodge them from the positions they now occupy, *but her Majesty's Government consider that the further advance of Russians should, subject to military considerations, be resisted by the Afghans.*" The result was that a series of collisions took place between the Russians and the Afghans on the river Murghab, culminating in the Russian attack on Pandjeh, of which place they obtained possession after a courageous resistance on the part of the Afghan defenders, who suffered heavy loss. Pandjeh having succumbed, the Russians proceeded to establish a temporary administration, to include also the surrounding districts. Hereupon England awoke to the fact that it was time to interfere, and accordingly preparations were made for war. After a time of suspense, however, the difficulty was ended by the Tsar agreeing to submit the matter to arbitration if desired; and finally a line of frontier was agreed upon which, with the exception that Pandjeh was exchanged for Zulfikar, was practically the same as that proposed by the Russians in January of 1885, and at that time rejected by the Gladstonian Ministry. Even after this, however, numerous complications ensued, and it was only with the greatest difficulty that a fresh frontier line on the north-west of Afghanistan was finally arrived at.

This matter at last settled, for the time being at any rate, Russia proceeded to see what could be done in the Pamirs, where the boundary lines were also but vaguely defined. For a time some anxiety was felt in England at this latest Russian movement, but was easily allayed by an "assurance" from that country on the subject. Whatever she means to do in that direction, however, it is an open secret that she regards the Hindu Kush as the proper boundary of British activity in Asia—that is to say, for the present—and that, centring her attention for the time being on obtaining a port on the Persian Gulf, or rather Indian Ocean, she looks upon an occupation of Herat as by no means a remote possibility. As has already been said, she has now extended her line of railway to within seventy miles of that town, and it is far from likely that the present terminus at Kushk will long remain the terminus.* On all hands it is admitted that the Merv-Kushk Railway is but a means to an end, and that end the establishment of Russian domination at Herat and in Northern Afghanistan generally. Nor is this line destined to be the only one having this important object. Already the country in the direction of Balkh has been carefully surveyed, and plans submitted to the Imperial authorities for a line of rail to that place, whilst the whole of the surrounding country has been so carefully studied that the position of almost every tree and hedge is known. At the same time, employing Askhabad as a centre, a network of Russian intrigue and acquisition is also being gradually spread further and further to the south of Persia, in preparation for the time when that country also can be easily absorbed. It is an understood thing that a railway is eventually to branch off towards the south from

* Written before the extension of the line beyond Kushk now in course of construction.

Askhabad, and thus, according to Russian writers themselves, open a way to the establishment of the Tsar's supremacy on the shores of the Persian Gulf and the Indian Ocean—"to be beforehand with the Germans," they say.

It is at present claimed for the Merv-Kushk Railway that it is merely a civilizing project; but it is well here to recall the words applied to the Central Asian Railway by Skobeleff. He declared that not for a generation or more would Russia be able to advance beyond Herat upon India. "But," he went on to say, "in the mean time, by this railway of ours, we are assuming a menacing position towards England, which will keep her occupied in India, and prevent her impeding us in other parts of the world." Clearly, then, if this line has any civilizing aim at all, that is by no means its sole purpose of creation.

The inevitable conclusion to be drawn from a study of the persistent Muscovite advance is that Russia will continue her encroachments. As has been demonstrated, she has now almost reached the very heart of Afghanistan, thus reducing the space intervening between herself and the frontiers of Britain's Asiatic Empire to comparatively insignificant proportions; but it is not to be supposed that, having reached this point, she has achieved the goal of her ambition. It may be asserted that, so long as she is not in possession of Herat, India is safe. But Herat is not impregnable, and it is obvious that the frontier line delimitated immediately after the Pandjeh incident places Russia in a position which would render the seizure of that town a comparatively easy matter, whenever she may arrive at the conclusion that such a *coup de main* is in other ways practicable. It, therefore, behoves Britain to carefully consider the present position of affairs, and to formulate and carry out some consistent line of policy which shall effectually protect her vast Eastern Empire from the Russian menace. Dangers are accumulating thick and fast on the frontier and in the adjacent countries, and the time has come for the British Government to make a determined stand, once and for all, against Russian interference in Afghanistan. A Russian occupation of Herat would not only be a direct menace in itself, but, if allowed, would give rise amongst the peoples of Afghanistan and India to an impression that England feared to oppose the Russians. Such a belief would lead to the most serious results. Even as it is, the Afghans could scarcely be depended upon to remain staunch allies, for they would naturally wait to discover the winning side; and any sign of weakness on the part of England would not only injure her best interests with them, but would alienate many who might be already vacillating in India itself. Nor should the fact be lost sight of that Herat is not the only danger point; for a part of the scheme for the projected railway from Askhabad to the Persian Gulf is to carry a branch line to Seistan and Nasratabad. The most sanguine believer in Russian "assurances" cannot by any possibility ascribe the construction of such a line to a desire for commercial development. On the other hand, it is a significant fact that this branch railway will provide the means of approach to the two routes from the Helmund valley to Kandahar, a city from which the Russians are at present some five hundred miles distant. The time has gone by for paying attention to pledges; it has been abundantly proved that they are given merely as a matter of diplomacy, and are abandoned whenever it is found convenient. The present position is one calling for careful consideration and decided action.

Assuming that the Russian advance towards India continues until the overstepping of a certain fixed line makes war inevitable, the British nation has to decide where that line is to be. No one is likely now to maintain that such a line will have been reached with the occupation of Herat or Balkh. Otherwise this occupation (not merely possible, but probable) would at once mean war. Is Britain prepared to go to war on such an account? and is she in a position to do so? If, then, not at Herat and Balkh, where is the line to be drawn? If Russia be allowed to occupy either or both of these places without opposition, should Britain make a corresponding counter-advance? and, if so, how far? or should she remain where she is, and complete, so far as the resources of India permit, her frontier defences, leaving Russia to gradually absorb Afghanistan? How about the engagement with the Amir to defend the integrity of Afghanistan? These are problems which we have to solve, nor can the solution of them be relegated to a future generation.

We have now to examine the chief factors in the case; the position of India for offence and defence, of Russia for offence, and the part likely to be played by Afghanistan and Persia, especially should either Russia or England, or both, occupy portions of these countries. Before arriving at any definite conclusion as to the probable ultimate result of these factors, the condition of India, Russia, Afghanistan, and Persia must be glanced at, whilst, at the same time, the position of China must always be borne in mind.

CHAPTER III

CENTRAL ASIA

Country and People

In order to acquire a comprehensive and clear idea of the part now being played in the world's history by the peoples of Central Asia, and to estimate with some degree of accuracy the possibilities attendant on the ever-progressing incursion into her territories of Western nations, it is necessary to consider, at some length, the various characteristics of climate, races, customs, and other important factors in the problem.

The climate of Central Asia varies considerably from the north to the south, and may be roughly divided into three zones. The northern zone extends as far south as latitude 45°, and includes the lower course of the Syr Daria to Fort No. 2, and the lower course of the Ili. The climate in this zone is what is known as "continental," with very hot summers and very cold winters. Snow remains on the ground for about three months, while the summer is extremely hot, and lasts from four to five months. The central zone includes the towns of Perovsky, Turkistan, Aulie-ata, and Vierny, with the middle course of the Syr Daria and a large portion of the Kyzyl Kum sands. Here the winter may be compared to that of Central Germany, while at Vierny grapes ripen, though not so well as further south. The southern zone is tropical, and includes Kuldja, besides those towns which lie either in the same latitude or south of Tashkent. Kuldja owes its comparatively high temperature to its sheltered position, being surrounded by high mountains, which protect it from the north-easterly winds so prevalent in the rest of the central zone. Fruits of a delicate nature flourish—peaches, apricots, pomegranates, and grapes. The winter though cold is short, snow seldom remaining on the ground for longer than a month. There is, however, a great deal of rain, the rainy season lasting from about March till October.

Besides these three rough divisions, in all the mountain valleys south of latitude 42°, and in the district of Hodjent, the winter is even shorter and the summer very hot. The pistachio tree can grow, and the wild peach, wild almond, and wild apple flourish, at a height of 4000 to 6000 feet above the level of the sea. The district of Hodjent, acquired by Russia in 1874, lies south of Tashkent, and with the valley of Zarafshan is the most fertile part of Central Asia. It was for some time a disputed point between Bokhara and Khokand. The country here is better wooded than most parts of Central Asia, and also better watered; everywhere one sees the beautiful gardens which are the joy and pride of all dwellers in Central Asian towns. These gardens surround most of the cities, and are often used as summer residences, the Russians even having adopted the fashion, and camping out in roomy tents and pavilions during the hot months. Peach, cherry, and apple trees make these gardens beautiful, and it is much to be regretted that, owing to the scarcity of coal, these orchards are being largely cut down for fuel.

With regard to mineral produce, the lack of good coal in Central Asia is likely to prove a serious drawback to its development, although the improvement in communications will largely remedy the defect. Since the acquisition of Turkistan, the Government have made great efforts to discover really productive coal-beds; but although coal exists scattered pretty widely over Central Asia, all that has been obtained hitherto is of inferior quality, and broken up into small fields. As for other minerals, it is curious, considering the trifling amount of gold found in this part of Russia's new possessions, that her first step towards Asia was initiated by Peter the Great because he had heard so much of the gold to be found on the banks of the Oxus. Lead-ore is the most abundant mineral, but this cannot be mined with any great profit on account of the dearness of fuel and difficulty of transport.

There are several different races inhabiting Central Asia, but, broadly speaking, they are all of Persian or Turkish descent. A part of the country was undoubtedly inhabited in early times by the Sacæ, or Scythians, an Aryan race who were to a large extent dispossessed and driven out by the Turkish tribes who overran the country. The descendants of this ancient race are still found in considerable numbers, often clustered together in mountain villages, to which they have been gradually driven by the succeeding waves of Turkish invasion. A curious testimony to the antiquity of the race is the fact that their language retains many words of Aryan derivation which are not known in modern Persian. The Tadjiks, as they are called, are distinguished, not only in appearance, but in character, from the tribes of Turkish descent. The typical Tadjik is large, thickly bearded, vain with the childish vanity common in primitive races, lazy, untruthful, and morally corrupt. He despises his less subtle Uzbek neighbour, who returns the sentiment, but is nevertheless compelled to make use of the sharper wit of the Tadjik. The Uzbeks, who form a large proportion of the population in Central Asia, are a tribe, or congeries of tribes, of much the same origin as the Kirghiz, being founded by Turkish immigrants who flocked into the country both before and after the time of Genghiz Khan. Unlike the Kirghiz, however, the Uzbeks have little of the Mongol element. They speak a Turkic dialect, and retain, at all events traditionally, their old division into clans or families, the names of which in some cases perpetuate long-forgotten tribes. One clan is that of the

Kiptchaks, whose martial habits and traditions made them a chief factor in the army of Khokand. The most numerous race, in the western part of Central Asia at all events, is the Kirghiz, also perhaps the most interesting.

This tribe really consists of two distinct races: the true one, the *Kara* or "Black Kirghiz," is found principally in the valleys of the Thian-Shan and Altai Mountains, and is unmistakably of Turkish origin. Descriptions found in Chinese writings of a very early date show that at that time the prevailing type was characterized by light hair and fair skin, which would not apply to the average Kirghiz of the present day, although such may still be met with here and there.

The other race, which inhabits the greater part of the province of Turkistan and the steppes bordering it, called by the Russians "Kassak-Kirghiz," * is more impregnated with the Mongol element than the Kara-Kirghiz race. They have largely intermarried with the Kalmuks, and their aristocracy, or "white bones," claim descent from Genghiz Khan, while their

* The word "Kirghiz" has practically the same derivation as the Russian "Cossack," and means "a wanderer."

various traditions describe them as being descended from a "red-haired dog," or (a more poetical story) as veritable "Children of the Mist." Both legends suggest the great antiquity of the race, being usual with aboriginal tribes of undoubted pre-historic origin, both in America and Australia. The claim of descent from an animal is found with other Asiatic tribes, and is always supposed to denote considerable age. Early travellers seem to have heard the legend, and translated it with more picturesqueness than veracity into actual fact; for in the description of a journey through this country made by the Christian king Hethum of Armenia, in the thirteenth century, we have a thrilling account of a race of which the men had the shape of dogs. This story is repeated by an Italian traveller, Carpini, and is also found, very circumstantially, in the Chinese encyclopedia, where the country is called "The Kingdom of Dogs."

Although he has now lost his independence, the Kirghiz still retains many curious and characteristic traits, one of these being an incurable contempt for a settled or town life. "Sart," the term applied to merchants and townsfolk, is used contemptuously, and would be much resented by a true Kirghiz, who has a scoffing proverb to the effect that "when a Sart becomes rich he builds a house, a Kirghiz buys more wives." When on the move they live in *kibitkas*, or felt tents, stretched on light wooden frames, and resembling the Mongolian *yourtas*. These *kibitkas* are exceedingly portable, and can be packed for a journey in less than an hour. The Kirghiz, as a rule, are of swarthy complexion, and are short and sturdy in build, the men shaving the head, but allowing the beard to grow, while the women wind yards of cotton stuff about their heads. The male attire consists usually of a pair of baggy leather breeches, a coarse shirt, and one or more rough coats, the head being covered with a skull-cap and a conical hood of sheepskin or felt. On special occasions a red velvet coat and a tall felt hat, with turned-up brim, are worn by the well-to-do. Polygamy was adopted by the race at the time when the Russians forced Mohammedanism upon them, and the position of their women-folk is not enviable. When a man wishes to marry he buys a wife, or one is bought for him by his relations, and once the *kalym*, or purchase-money, is paid, the wife becomes the mere chattel of her husband, who generally treats her with less consideration than he does his cattle. He can divorce her with the greatest ease, and her family may then attempt to sell her again. However much she may be ill-treated she has no redress, the utmost that can happen being a remonstrance from her relations to the husband for "depreciating her market value;" whilst, even if he killed her, under Kirghiz law he had no more serious penalty to encounter than a fine. "A woman has only half as much soul as a man," says a Kirghiz proverb; and the men of the tribe evidently act up to this belief. The more serious crimes are now amenable to Russian law, but smaller matters are settled before certain chosen elders, who are not paid for their services, but receive a portion of every fine they inflict. Hitherto little has been done by Russia to civilize the tribes under her dominion, and such a thing as a Kirghiz school is practically unknown. Although Mohammedanism is nominally their religion, the Kirghiz do not trouble much about doctrine, many of them still adhering to the old *Shaman*, or devil-worship, while ancestor-worship is still largely practised. When a man of importance dies, two camels, led by priests, are placed on either side of the corpse, and a form is repeated, transferring the sins of the dead man to the camels, which then become the property of the priests. This is only one of many curious customs connected with funerals, and marriage ceremonies are equally interesting and numerous. It may be said, perhaps, that the principal object of Kirghiz existence is the breeding of cattle and horses, to which nearly the whole of their time is devoted. In bartering his cattle the Kirghiz does not make a feature of honesty, and will inevitably cheat whenever he gets the chance.

Fond as he is of horse-flesh, his sheep—of which he has a famous fat-tailed breed called the *Kurdiak*—are perhaps nearest to the heart of the Kirghiz. All over Central Asia, and in Southern Siberia, mutton is the staple food, and the nomads who inhabit the steppe regions are accustomed to eat it in tremendous quantities. The allowance for a Mongol driver of a caravan, for instance, is a leg of mutton per man per day; but it must be added that, should meat fail, the Mongol is not only capable of foregoing his favourite food, but of existing on fare so coarse and scanty that no European could support life on it. The nomads, as a rule, do not take much trouble over the preparation of their food, boiling it in a pot, and taking it out in handfuls as it seems to them sufficiently cooked, or gnawing the flesh from the bones, which they return to the pot again. A very delicate dish, and one set before honoured guests, is composed of the tails of sheep; and the shin-bone of this useful animal is carried by superstitious Kirghiz as an amulet, and is also used in divination, as described elsewhere. His sheep are, indeed, so important to the Kirghiz or Uzbek, or to any native of Central Asia, that it is etiquette to suppose, for the sake of courtesy, that every man possesses flocks, and in greeting him the first inquiry must be not for *his* health but for *theirs*.

The favourite drink of the Kirghiz is made from brick-tea; but *kumis*, or mares' milk, is drunk, as among the Mongols, to produce intoxication, for which purpose also is used a kind of beer, distilled from grain, called *buza*, which has a stupefying effect.

On the whole, the Kirghiz are a simple and credulous people, not particularly brave.

Owing to their skill as trackers, in which they rival the Red Indians, they make excellent scouts. Politically, their great importance must be acknowledged ; for, to quote again the words of the Great Tsar, their land is "the key and gate to all the countries of Asia."

The Kalmuks, with whom, as has been said, the Kirghiz have largely intermarried, are another race of Central Asian nomads, who originated in a confederacy of Mongol tribes living in Zungaria, on the north-western borders of the Chinese Empire, and combining together to resist the aggressions of another tribe of kindred origin. This confederacy, known as the Oirat, made attacks on China, and at one time took the Emperor prisoner, and marched to the walls of Peking. Internal dissensions, however, broke the power of the Oirat, and some of the tribes migrated to Siberia, probably receiving at that time the name of "Kalmuk," which in Turkic dialect means "remnant." Zungaria still remained in the possession of the same tribes, whose fratricidal wars and quarrels finally ended in their becoming vassals to China. Meanwhile, the Kalmuks had been driven further and further, till finally they crossed the Ural, and settled in the lower region of the Volga. Finding her new subjects in Zungaria inclined to rebel, China took a short way of quieting them by a wholesale massacre, and as the country was left desolate, towards the middle of the eighteenth century military colonies of Manchus were formed and Chinese criminals sent, while large numbers of agriculturists were deported from Eastern Turkistan. The last-named became known as *tarantchis*, and occupied a position analogous to that of Russian crown peasants. Although Mohammedans, they lived among their Buddhist neighbours quite amicably, and the only difference made by the preponderance of the Chinese element was in the unveiling of their women. Another element was added in 1771, when the Kalmuks, hearing that their mother-country had been depopulated, returned *en masse*, taking eight months on the journey, and suffering much both from want and the attacks of the Kirghiz. When they arrived they found the country occupied by the Chinese, and having no alternative, except to fall into the hands of Kirghiz or Russians, they settled down on the pasture lands, became subject to the Chinese, and devoted themselves to the breeding of cattle and horses. The Kalmuks are all Buddhists, and are completely Mongolian in type and customs. This district, known, from the name of the Manchu settlement which dominated it, as Kuldja, was annexed by Russia, but returned to China on her fulfilling certain conditions.

On the western side of Central Asia there are many different families or tribes of Turkomans, who are somewhat similar in habits to the Kirghiz, although some, like the Tekkés, live partly in villages and are agriculturists. No race offered more stubborn resistance to the Russians than the Tekkés, and none suffered more. In the Turkoman campaigns orders were given to spare neither age nor sex, and whole families were slaughtered and entire districts laid waste.

In most of the cities of Central Asia, besides these, are found many fragments of other races—Persians, originally brought as slaves; Arabs, believed by some to have been the original introducers of Mohammedanism; Hebrews, who have been settled in the country for centuries, and who have the characteristics for which their race is remarkable all over the world; Hindoos, who come and go for commercial purposes; and also many families of gipsies, known usually as Liuli, who lead a nomad life, trading in horses, while their women tell fortunes, cure the sick, and carry on a small traffic.

The Trans-Caucasus is inhabited by various races—Georgians, Mingrelians, Gurians, Kuchetians, and others, all living from the oldest times under sovereign princes who embraced Christianity at an early period. These voluntarily became dependants of Russia, when they found themselves unable to repel unaided the attacks of the wild mountaineer tribes of the Caucasus or the incursions of Persian tyrants and robbers. Besides the native races, Tartars, Kurds, Turks, Persians, Russians, Germans, Frenchmen, and Jews are settled in the Caucasus, and it is said that in this district no less than 68 languages are spoken, while the whole of Russia includes only 115. As previously noted, the troops of the Caucasus are composed of the pick of the Russian army. The romantic and gorgeous country, the strange customs of the people, and the generally excellent conditions of the garrisons, make the life an agreeable one; and in former days there was always some sort of small war going on, or an expedition against robbers, which kept the Caucasian soldier on the *qui vive.* The variability of the climate inures him to both heat and cold.

The Cossack troops of the Caucasus are composed of the pick of the Russian regular army, whilst officers of every nation are found in its ranks. It may be incidentally mentioned here that the Cossacks (originally known as "Kazaks," *i.e.* wanderers, freebooters) are a mixed race of Russians, Poles, Tartars, and others, who originally came from the south and south-east of Russia. They have always been of a warlike character, and were at one time divided into two clans, the Don and the Dnieper Cossacks, both being independent of the Imperial Government. The Dnieper Cossacks, however, in 1652 tendered their allegiance to the Tsar, whilst the Don Cossacks became Russian subjects during the time of Ivan the Terrible, the foundation of the Cossack army of the Ural being laid in 1613–14, when specified territories were offered to them on condition of certain military services.

Every male Cossack who is fit is bound to military service during war. From the age of seventeen he is liable to *stanitza** duty, and from his twentieth year to regimental duty. Formerly the term of service was for life, the Cossack being exclusively a soldier from his birth; but the lifelong service has now been reduced to from twenty to twenty-five years. The conscription is made in each *stanitza*, and those who escape pay a tax for the period of obligatory service. The Cossack soldier provides horse and equipment at his own expense, for which he receives an allowance from the crown. Every tribe, in addition, is granted so much land to support themselves and their flocks, and every Cossack possesses land in ratio to his military rank.

The Cossacks in the Orenburg district have no fixed quarters, but are constantly moving about, and patrol the most remote corners of the district. The Ural Cossacks are the descendants of the old fighting race, which, in the time of Peter the Great, made the first dash into Central Asia; the Orenburg Cossack are a different type, and are descended from the more peaceful colonists, who were sent to protect the fortresses after they had been built. They have more

* Cossack posts or settlements.

regular habits, and care more for home-life and agricultural pursuits, so do not make such dashing soldiers as their cousins the Ural Cossacks. The latter are far more popular among the troops of Central Asia.

The Orenburgers, moreover, are a mixed race, for when, in 1755, an ukase ordered the organization of a Cossack army in the newly formed province of Orenburg, the population was so sparse that Don Cossacks, broken and impoverished noblemen from Poland and Russia, and, in fact, any wastrels who could be found, were induced to settle there—indeed, whole villages of Tartars were persuaded to migrate. This introduction of fresh blood was not very successful, and efforts were made to get rid, at all events, of the Tartar element.

Of late years education has been more carefully attended to; but until 1858 there was no sort of examination for non-commissioned officers. During the sixties several schools were established, private and military, and a cadet school at Orenburg, which gives a purely military education. The measures adopted did not, however, seem conducive to the military spirit which the Government desires to foster, and, since then, further steps have been taken. The comparative peaceableness of the times gave the young soldier little practical experience. In all the schools the martial spirit is now carefully cultivated, and there is generally an old Cossack veteran who drills and exercises the children. It was not until 1803 that a particular uniform for the whole army was ordered. This has undergone various modifications, but now consists of dark green coat and pantaloons—the Ural Cossacks having red facings, red-striped breeches, and red *kolpaks*. The breeches are tucked into high boots, a grey cavalry pelisse is worn, and a fur cap, known as the *papacha*, with blue or red *kolpak*.

In fighting with the Kirghiz, and other tribes in Central Asia, the usual mode of procedure of the Cossacks is to link their horses into a circle, and, kneeling behind them, to fire, not in volleys but in files, upon their opponents, picking off the leaders. It has been said that "the roll of glorious deeds accomplished in Poland, in Turkistan, and in the Kirghiz steppe, bear eloquent testimony to the great moral force the Cossacks possess;" but much more, we may add, to their obstinate courage, which makes them willing to die, but not to accept defeat.

There is a Caucasian Militia corps, recruited for the most part from Georgian or Tartar volunteers, and also irregular cavalry regiments, such as the Daghestan horse, which took part in the Khivan campaign. A squadron of these volunteer mountaineers, in their picturesque national costume, forms the showy Circassian bodyguard of the Tsar.

Alexandropol and Achalzych are the only fortresses according to modern ideas—the posts in the mountains were not built to resist guns. Generally they consist only of walled towers for the guns, connected by walls with loopholes, in the centre of which enclosure stands the commander's house, with the wells and store-house. Sometimes they consist merely of a single tower, and the guns, generally antiquated, are protected by a wooden roof, or even lie unmounted on the ground.*

* The steppe forts are constructed according to one of the following methods: (1) A small redoubt, holding about one hundred men, with two barbettes, and with powder magazines in the thickness of the parapet. The redoubt, placed to command the barracks, which are built outside, serves as a keep; the walls of the barracks (made of sun-dried bricks), where facing the country, are pierced with loopholes. Sometimes a flank defence is provided by throwing up a lunette, with a barbette. (2) A quadrangle, with outer walls loopholed, in which are barracks, hospital, commissariat depôt, etc., and within the space enclosed by the quadrangle are

On the Central and Lower Terek still remain some of the old Cossack watch-houses—small redoubts, with a wooden house for the accommodation of the garrison (often only from ten to twenty Cossacks). Near this is a raised wooden platform on which a sentry marches up and down. Their duties are now purely of a private and police nature, but in old times these were posts of great danger, for, when the mountaineers swooped down suddenly, the Cossacks could only give the alarm by fire to the next post, and were often surrounded and killed despite the most obstinate resistance.

In the Caucasus the peasantry, even when following agricultural pursuits, are invariably armed with sabre, dagger, or ancient gun.

Theoretically nearly all the native peoples of Central Asia profess Mohammedanism, but many of the tribes know little more of it than the name of the prophet, and some not even that. The nomads retain many practices which have no connection with Islam, and it is only in the large cities that there is any attempt at ceremonial worship. Great religious laxity prevails

the uninhabited buildings—stables, sheds, armouries, etc. Lunettes are provided, furnishing artillery and musketry defence to the forces of the fort.

all over Central Asia, and the fanaticism observable among the Dervishes, who gain a living by exhibiting themselves in a religious frenzy and even torturing themselves at times, is rather a matter of business than of true devotion.

Education among the native inhabitants is in the hands of the *mullahs*, or priests, and is generally limited to such matters as have a bearing on religion or law. The foundation of colleges, where the higher religion and law are taught, has for ages been a favourite form of piety, and some still exist which were founded four and five hundred years ago. Both pupils and professors are supported from the revenues of the college, the latter receiving in addition voluntary gifts from parents of the pupils. There are also primary schools, generally attached to each mosque; and here the boys from the age of five are instructed first in the alphabet, and then in the reading of the Koran and about seven other books, which they read and copy without understanding, as they are written in Persian and Turki and never translated into the dialect of the district. To know the Koran by heart confers at once rank and sanctity on the happy accomplisher of that feat. This is usually an effort entirely of memory, as few are acquainted with Arabic, though many have read illegal translations and know the substance of what they recite. Superstition is extremely rife, especially among the nomad tribes, who attach mystic meaning to such events as the appearance of crows (as in Western Europe), magpies, and other birds and beasts. A favourite method of divination is by roasting the shin-bone of a sheep and watching its appearance as it burns, from which the future is predicted by certain signs. Such a bone is also carried as an amulet.

As regards religion, the Russians have always acted with the greatest wisdom and tolerance, never in any way interfering with the worship and practice of the conquered tribes, except that they have abolished the native functionaries whose business was to compel the performance of religious rites. Missionary projects have been by no means encouraged, although in the garrisons and in one or two towns there are Christian churches, and a Bishop of the province of Turkistan. The Russians have acted with less wisdom in arranging the administration of their new provinces; and, in trying to force upon the natives systems foreign to their customs and characters, they have earned a great deal of unpopularity. One instance is the method of local government by natives elected by vote, under the surveillance of the Russian Government. This, with modifications, has been tried among Kirghiz, Uzbeks, and in the chief towns. The people left to themselves would always elect men of influence and popularity—their former leaders,—who, for obvious reasons, are not acceptable to the Russians; so that the system has degenerated into mere farce, and is viewed with contempt by the natives, the men chosen being merely the tools of Government.

The native mind, especially at first, found Russian taxes and laws extremely difficult of comprehension, more especially as the former were constantly changed, according to the will and pleasure of the prefect of the particular district, or, indeed, of any official who happened to be in charge. Nor were the officials in Turkistan of a high order. Very often they had been sent there because their reputation was not good enough to secure them home appointments, and venality and corruption do not escape the eyes of observant natives. Nor has official Russia always kept her promises or acted with strict honesty towards her vassals. In the Khivan campaign, for instance, 8800 camels were commandeered for the army from the Kirghiz in different districts, and these were to be paid for at the rate of fifty roubles each if they died. As nearly all perished a large sum was due to the Kirghiz, but the Prefect of Perovsky, thinking this a good opportunity to show his zeal, bullied and threatened the people into signing an address which made the camels a present to the Government, which would, he said, never pay for them anyhow! The result was that the people felt that they had been robbed of their camels—their one possession.

CHAPTER IV

CENTRAL ASIA

COUNTRY AND PEOPLE—*continued*

THE advent of the Russians in Central Asia has naturally made a great difference in many of the towns, which, originally entirely Oriental in character and appearance, now present the curious contrast of European streets and squares, occupied by officials and their families in the unpicturesque garb of the Western world, side by side with the native towns, old, in some cases, with an age which makes such cities as York mere infants; trodden by countless generations of conquerors—Macedonians, Scythians, Arabs, Persians, Mongols,—and which have succumbed—is it for ever?—to a greater than these, a race from the West.

The further one penetrates into the heart of Asia the less has this modernizing influence made itself felt; so that between Orenburg, which is really on the borders of civilization, and Samarkand there is a wide gulf.

Perhaps one of the most typical towns under the new *régime* is Tashkent, the capital of the province of Turkistan and a city of very ancient origin. Mention is made in the seventh century by a Chinese traveller of a city, either on the same spot, or near the site of the present one, called Tchatch or Jadj. This name, difficult of pronunciation to the Persians, who became later masters of the place, was probably altered to Shash—"kent" being merely a Persian word for town. The Turkish nomad tribes, who are the ancestors of many of the present inhabitants, would find no meaning in the word "Shash," which they in all probability altered to "Tash," a stone; and so the city bears in its name a record of the many hands through which it has passed.

Briefly its history up to a certain point is the story of the struggle between the two sovereigns of Bokhara and Samarkand, and when both were subdued by the Tartar chief, Genghiz Khan, it remained in the possession of his descendants until reconquered by a Khan who ruled over both Bokhara and Samarkand. Then came the Kirghiz, who held it for more than a hundred years, till it fell before an enterprising ruler of Zungaria, and, after a short time, achieved a semi-independence, being alternately overlorded by Khokand and Bokhara. It was in the struggle with Khokand that General Tchernaieff, fearing that Tashkent would fall into the hands of the hostile Amir of Bokhara, to whom the inhabitants—between Scylla and Charybdis—had appealed for help, invested the place with a comparatively small army, and, being fortunate enough to kill the Regent of Khokand in the first engagement and to cut off the water-supply of the city, entered by two gates simultaneously, chased the Khokandians and Bokharans out of the city, and received the unconditional surrender of the natives. The Russian rule was firmly established, and order maintained by native police, who still seem to work well under their new masters.

A Russian colony, with the Governor-General in his palace as the centre, and the usual military and civil officials and their families, has now its own quarter, side by side with the quaint Oriental town of Tashkent. The little houses of Russian merchants and officials are whitewashed, trim, and neat; the governor's palace has an ornamental garden round it, laid out in artificial lakes and little hills and dales, where a military band plays every evening. There are stiff public buildings, a wide square, an ugly little church, and a new improved bazaar has been erected at great cost, which has, however, entirely failed in its object of drawing the trade of the town from the native quarter, and so subjecting it more completely to Government influence. The natives did not take kindly to this arrangement, and the trade of Tashkent is still carried on in the old bazaar, which has probably existed in much the same form for hundreds of years.

The bazaar is a most important feature of life in all Oriental countries, and, as all bazaars in Central Asia have a family likeness, that of Tashkent will serve as a very fair type. No changes or improvements have been effected in it since the Russian occupation. The street, as the gate is neared, grows narrower, and little shops cluster on either side; in the bazaar itself it is exceedingly narrow, rough, and ill-paved. A very favourite method of paving in Central

Asia is by laying large blocks of stone, between which are channels of mud in winter, and in summer of thick white dust. Over these the Kirghiz bumps along on his camel, quite unconcerned, and if the pedestrian does not keep carefully to the raised side-walk of mud he may be knocked over or jostled by these camels. The shops are small wooden huts of one or, at most, two rooms, the front of which is taken down bodily to show the interior. In the centre, on a mat, the seller sits cross-legged, or perhaps it is a manufacturer with his tools in hand. Round him are displayed his wares, and there is little room for his customers, who must stand outside to do their bargaining. One thinks of the unfortunate man in the Arabian Nights, who bought a tray of china, set it down before him in his shop, and, while meditating on the fortune he should make out of it, fell asleep, and, dreaming of his future glories, kicked out and over went the china!—his castle in Spain falling about his ears with a crash. One would not be surprised to hear that such events are a daily occurrence, but then there is none of the hurry and bustle of European shopping. The merchant displays no undue eagerness to sell his goods, and the buyer is equally self-possessed and leisurely. Theoretically there are thirty-two different trade guilds, which must be represented in the bazaar; practically there are more. Each guild is supposed to have thirty-two branches, and each must have a different shop; thus, in brass-working (sometimes very beautifully done) one shop will make the bowl or ewer, another the bottom, another the lid, a fourth will solder them together, while at a fifth, with a sharp chisel, the decoration is worked out. Almost every trade has its own street, the shops on either side being devoted to shoe, or harness, or crockery-making in all their different branches.

At a tea-shop, sometimes kept by a dancing-boy, tea only can be obtained, and the natives bring their own bread, or little round cakes which they can buy at a neighbouring baker's shop, and which they fold up in a corner of their girdle, and spread out, using the girdle as a tablecloth, when they desire to eat.

The jewellers have a little furnace and bellows, and a few rude instruments, with which they manufacture ear-rings, amulets, and anklets, generally in silver or thin gold, set with turquoises or other stones of an inferior quality. Some of the merchants have wooden booths with awnings, and there are innumerable itinerant vendors standing about the streets. Our own ice-cream man finds his counterpart in an individual who sells a sort of powdery white sugar to boys for a trifling sum, while in a small clearing, perhaps, is a crowd of grinning Sarts watching the antics of a couple of comedians. The Kirghiz have a special quarter of their own in the great bazaar of Tashkent, and here is sold the really beautiful felt made by the women, also coarse carpets and other articles of nomad manufacture. Here and there are arched gateways, behind which are caravanseries, some used by local merchants for storing their goods, and others as hostelries for foreigners. Here the merchandise lies about in piles, the camels and horses stabled around the sides of the court, while overhead the merchants "live, move, and have their being" in an atmosphere which is, luckily, peculiar to bazaars.

Every Mussulman city, to be *en règle*, must have a "Jumma," or mosque large enough to hold all the inhabitants on Friday. Looking from the platform of the mosque in Tashkent (whence the mullah calls to prayers), one sees apparently nothing but a flat clay plain, beyond which rises a hill with another mosque, and the domed roof of a bath. This plain is composed of the mud roofs of the bazaar, for the streets are so narrow that one can only see them from below, and as the roofs are often overgrown with grass and poppies, this adds to the illusion. The barber's shop is also the chemist's, and here soap—very unpleasant in smell—is sold, and also the cosmetics which a good Mussulwoman is enjoined to use in order to preserve her beauty and so please her husband.

The natives of Tashkent are mostly Uzbeks, with a few Tadjiks, Tartars, Kirghiz, Hindoos, and others who come to trade. The population is difficult to gauge, but is probably over 120,000.

The Hindoos are the great money-lenders of Central Asia, and have their own caravanseries in most towns, but under Russian rule, unlike that of the English in India, land does not pass by sale and mortgage into their hands. The Jews are also numerous, and have enjoyed greater freedom (little though that be now) since the advent of the Russians. Formerly they were confined to a certain quarter, and treated with much contempt, having very few civil or municipal rights, and being compelled to wear a girdle of common rope as a badge of their nationality.

Cotton and silk goods, of course, occupy a large portion of the bazaar, and in the booths one can see the men at work with their rough machines of wood, dexterously manipulating reels and turning spindles. The embroidery of robes is also done by men, and is in very great demand, the robe or material being stretched over a wooden hoop, the pattern roughly chalked, and the work executed with a kind of crochet-needle, with which the silken thread is pulled into a chain-stitch. There is no liquid measure in Central Asia, everything being reckoned by weight, and the standard varies in almost every town. The coins also, the most common of which is known as the *tenga,* have different values in different parts. The Russians have tried to regulate this, and are introducing their own money, which now passes current all over Central Asia.

The native houses of the better class in Tashkent, as in other Central Asian cities, have three, or at least two, courts. The first, if there are three, is used as a stable for the animals, which are accommodated in sheds round the sides. The second is the man's court, on two sides of which are the balconies of the house; while a third frequently has a sort of platform, used as a terrace, where the master and his friends sit to get the full benefit of the air. The house generally contains one large room, opening on the portico—the guest-chamber, with one or two smaller ones opening into it. The doors are often beautifully carved, and instead of hinges they hang on a sort of pivot let into the lintel and threshold. Windows, as a rule, there are none, but a small open space above the doors, with lattice-work let in, either open or covered with white paper, glass being still uncommon in the typical native house. The ceilings are very curious and sometimes strikingly pretty, being composed of small round willow boughs set in between the rafters, and picked out in colours, with an occasional touch of gold. The walls are plastered and frequently painted with pictures of fruit, flowers, or small arabesques, and there are numerous niches with arched tops which act as shelves, on which are stored books, clothes, crockery, or food. There is usually very little furniture, unless the merchant has become bitten with the craze to imitate the Russians, in which case there are cheap tables and chairs of a conventional type imported from Russia, for such things are not made in Tashkent. The truly native house, however, contains little but rugs and mattresses, with perhaps a small round table, or a carved or painted wooden cupboard. The women's quarters are very much the same in arrangement and furniture, except that they may have a broad bed—the *charpoy* of India—made of a wooden frame with a network of ropes, raised a few feet from the floor. The usual bed is merely a rug or a thin mattress stretched on the ground. In many of the rooms a small basin is let into a corner of the floor, with a jug standing by, for the numerous ablutions required by the Mussulman's religion. An honoured visitor to such a house as this is always treated to what is known as a *dostar khan* (literally, a tablecloth), which means that a piece of striped calico or silk is laid down, and dishes of sweetmeats or fruits are brought in and placed on it. A favourite dish consists of carrots chopped fine in honey, and little round cakes are much liked. The bread, which is thin and wafer-like, is baked by being plastered on the sides of a round oven.

The merchant who lives in this house is attired in a pair of loose white trousers made of cotton, and tied round his waist with a cord and tassels. His shirt, also of light-coloured cotton, is very long, with a small slit for the neck, and wide sleeves; over this he wears a *tchapan*, or two or three, according to the weather. This garment is a long coat, cut very sloping at the neck, and with enormous sleeves, much too long for convenience, but satisfying the Asiatic sense of propriety, which requires that the hands be covered. The *tchapan* is of cotton or silk in summer, often striped or patterned in the most gorgeous colours; in winter, one gown will be made of cloth and lined with fine sheepskin or fur. A scarf or small shawl is twisted round the waist, and a turban, either of striped cotton or, if the wearer is a *mullah* or distinguished for piety, of white material, is wound round the head over a little embroidered skull-cap.

The dress of the women is very similar, but their gowns are more often of silk, and many strings of beads, gold, and gems are worn round the neck, with bracelets, anklets, hair-ornaments, and sometimes nose-rings. Outside they wear a thick veil of woven horsehair, and a dark-blue or green cloak with long sleeves. The class of women who go abroad unveiled is such that even Jewesses and others, whose religion does not demand it, cannot venture out without these hideous garments. This applies, however, only to the purely Mussulman cities. In the east, where the Buddhist element is strong, an unveiled woman is not unknown, while the custom has never obtained among the Kirghiz and other nomad tribes, whose Mohammedanism is even less than skin deep.

Although there are hotels in Tashkent, and in many other Central Asian towns, they are by no means according to Western ideas of comfort, resembling in arrangement the caravanserai already described. The food of the country is mutton, mutton, mutton! In the town there is some attempt to vary the method of cooking; but, as a rule, the dishes are too greasy and insipid for European palates. Wine can be got in Tashkent, imported from Russia, at fabulous prices; but the native drink is green tea, black tea having been only introduced by the Russians, and this is sometimes thickened with cream or melted tallow, and sometimes flavoured with a small dried lemon.

The walls of Tashkent are said to have been sixteen miles round, but were largely demolished by the Russians, to make barracks and parade-grounds. Outside these walls and the gardens surrounding them is the open steppe, over which are dotted numerous villages, mostly inhabited by either Tartars or Kirghiz, the races who mingle in the city keeping apart here. One is a sort of summer residence for the governor and his little court, and at another is a large establishment for the breeding and improvement of horses, nominally a private enterprise, but in reality subsidized by Government, which realizes the importance of a plentiful supply of horses from a strategical point of view.

Altogether, Tashkent is a curious and typical example of East meeting West. The modern Russian soldier and his Paris-dressed wife rub shoulders with the Uzbek or Kirghiz, whose ancestors were Khans and Beks in this country at a time when Russia was a mere congeries of half-savage states; or with the Mongols, whose warrior kings in days of old not only conquered

Russia, but a great portion of the then known world; or with the Tadjiks, of almost prehistoric origin, former owners of the soil, who were dispossessed by Kirghiz and Mongol alike, but still retain their individuality. All these varying peoples have accepted the yoke of their Western conquerors. The Oriental is, above all, a fatalist, and he recognizes the inevitable wave of Russian advance. Once the White Tsar had proved his power, the Sart, at all events—for the nomads are less tractable—bowed his head and made the best of things. And such will be the case even in Afghanistan, as Russia moves forward towards India.

Another typical town, interesting from many points of view, but more especially the historical and antiquarian, is Samarkand, closely connected with the history of Alexander the Great. It first comes into notice as Maracanda, capital of Sogdiana, at the time of its capture by Alexander a large and flourishing city. Here he made his headquarters while he was subduing the mountain tribes, and during the celebrated expedition against the Scythians across the Syr Daria. This river was mistaken by the Macedonians for the Don, and so occasioned the well-known words of Alexander, "No more worlds to conquer!" He thought he had made the circuit of Asia and returned to Europe—a mistake which was imitated by later geographers out of compliment to the Macedonian conqueror. It was in Samarkand Alexander killed his friend Clytus in a drunken fit. In this district legends of Iskender Dulkarnian (the "two-horned," as he was called) abound, and the city of Alexandria which he founded is usually placed at Hodjent. Many of the petty princes in the mountain countries of the Upper Oxus claim descent from him, but very little trace remains of the Greek culture which he is said to have introduced. The dynasties which he founded in Central Asia, calling the two provinces Bactria and Sogdiana, lasted until about 130 B.C., when a nomad tribe known as the Yuetchi became masters of Samarkand, and were probably in possession of it when, in 710 A.D., the Arabs forcibly introduced Mohammedanism. For many years after, Samarkand remained a Christian See and had a bishop, and notwithstanding the successive conquests of the city by Persians, Turks, and eventually by Genghiz Khan, in the middle of the thirteenth century the Christians were still a flourishing community, while Marco Polo, though he did not personally visit the city, tells us that the Church of St. John the Baptist still existed. When Timur came and overthrew the dynasty of Genghiz, he made Samarkand his capital, and his tomb still remains, in a fairly good state of preservation, one of the most interesting sights of this interesting city. The great Baber, afterwards Emperor of India, made it a favourite resort, and his memoirs, written in the year 1497, have a glowing description of its beauties, more especially of the gardens, mosques, and palaces. An ambassador from King Henry of Castile, the good knight Don Roy Gonzalez de Clavijo, also gives a description of the magnificence of the city, but from his time onward little was known of it until its capture by the Russians in 1866. When and how the Christian community and religion so completely disappeared we do not know, but there are no remains of a Christian church. A small modern one has been built since the Russian occupation. A quaint story is told in connection with a high bare hill just outside Samarkand. When the original Arab missionaries were journeying to spread the doctrines of Mohammed, they stopped to rest on this hill, and cutting up and boiling a sheep (a method of divination which reminds one of the Kirghiz of the present day), they agreed to decide by lot their future destination. One drew out the head, which gave him the first choice, and he decided to remain at Samarkand; another, drawing the heart, desired to return to Mecca; while the third, getting the hind quarter, preferred to go to Bagdad,—hence Mecca is called the heart and Samarkand the head of Islam to this day. He who remained at Samarkand was given the name of Tchupanata, "Father Shepherd," and the hill is called after him to this day.

A curious relic, which reminds one of the famous Scone stone in the throne of Great Britain, is the Kok-tash, an oblong block of grey marble, ten feet four inches wide and two feet high. This is said to have served as the foundation for the throne of Timur, and Baber mentions the custom that every prince of the race of Timur had to be crowned on this throne. This custom grew into a superstition until it became a legend that the stone had fallen from heaven, and would allow none but those of the blood of Timur to sit on it. As late as 1772 the people rebelled against their Amir because he had not fulfilled this condition. The Russians have placed a brass railing round the stone to preserve it from too curious travellers, and the building in which it stands, once an Amir's palace, has been converted into a military hospital. Most of the beautiful mosques and other buildings in Samarkand, now in decay (among which must be mentioned the splendid Medressé, or College, built by the wife of Timur), bear distinct evidence of Persian influence, and the Persian lion adorns many of the interiors.

It is impossible to give any adequate descriptions of all the ancient and historic towns which have so recently fallen into the hands of Russia, but passing mention must be made of Turkistan, the town which has given its name to the province, originally a stronghold of Khokand and celebrated as containing the finest and most revered mosque in all Central Asia. It was a place of pilgrimage for people of the highest rank, and contains the tombs of many of the Kirghiz Khans of the Middle and Lesser Hordes. This mosque was begun by Timur in 1397, and is built over the tomb of one of the most celebrated saints in Asia, Hazret Hodja Akhmed Yasavi, who died about 1120 and is regarded by the Kirghiz as their patron saint. The great hall under the dome is over a hundred feet high, and decorated with alabaster work in the style common to Moorish buildings, such as the Alhambra. The whole mosque at one time must have been most beautifully decorated, but is much despoiled, both by earthquakes and by the hand of man. The Russians, when besieging Turkistan (or Hazret-i-Turkistan,* as it is called), directed their fire particularly at the mosque, which would have been entirely ruined, had not the Shiekh-ul-Islam, whose headquarters are here, mounted the parapets with a white flag. The town itself is poor and dirty, but Oriental in character, and therefore picturesque.

The town of Orenburg is the centre for trade between Russia and Central Asia, and as such is the gathering-place of all the nations engaged in it. It was founded in 1735, and since then has been twice transplanted. It is both European and Asiatic, possessing in one part elegant buildings, theatres, museums, palaces, restaurants, and

* Practically, "Sacred Turkistan"—Hazret meaning "presence" or "majesty" when applied to kings, or "sanctity" when referring to saints.

pleasure-gardens, where one may see in the evenings ladies, dressed in the latest Paris fashion, listening to the military band. In another part is the Cossack quarter, with low wooden houses, and broad, sandy, unpaved streets. Here Englishmen, Germans, Frenchmen, and Russians live peaceably together. On the south of the city stands a huge bazaar, which attracts all the tribes and nations of Central Asia. Kirghiz, Khivans, and Bokharians, in their strange native garb, wander through the streets, and one meets the cunning-looking Mongol and Bashkir, and the pious and subdued Persian.

CHAPTER V

CENTRAL ASIA

Country and People—*continued*

The Mohammedan religion, almost universal in Central Asia, gives little encouragement to those who seek pleasure and recreation, save in the exercise of religious duties and such mild excitement as learning to recite the Koran by heart. Human nature is, however, the same in the East as in the West, and the Bokharan, Khokandian, or Tashkentian, when he desires relaxation, turns to music and dancing, and even, if he is able, to horse-racing. As regards the first, the Russians of course, in such cities as Orenburg, have introduced military bands and American organs; but the purely native instruments are drums, variations of the zither and guitar, whose very names betray their relationship to the instruments familiar to us; trumpets, with perhaps one deep note, and some elementary wood wind instruments. The music is quite unlike our own, the intervals between the notes being less, and the notation consequently extremely varied. The effect is weird and unmelodious to the unaccustomed ear; but it is certainly more in keeping with the character and appearance of the natives than a Russian military band playing the latest opera selections. Most of the instruments, and probably much of the music, were brought from Persia, and the latter has retained its pristine rudeness of construction with a conservatism peculiar to these parts. Another instrument which is a great favourite, and found so generally all over the world that we are forced to believe it embodies some unspoken sentiment common to all mankind, is the Jew's harp, which bears here the very appropriate name of *tchang*. The nomad tribes, and particularly the Kirghiz, have mournful, monotonous songs of great length, some not at all unpleasing to the ear, which differ a good deal in style from the music of the towns, and probably owe their inspiration to the Mongol and not the Persian element.

The tambourine in different forms is much used, and is the favourite accompaniment to dancing. The latter is not really permitted to the true believer, nor are women allowed to appear in public and dance; but that does not interfere with the desire for a recreation which appeals to the sense of beauty and love of grace inherent in the most primitive race. Youths and boys are therefore trained to take the place of dancing-girls, and are a recognized institution all over Central Asia, although most in vogue in Bokhara and Samarkand. It was formerly the custom for every Bokharan gentleman of wealth to have one or more of these dancing-boys, or *batchas*, in his train of servants, while two or three men, if individually too poor to keep one, would club together in order to have a *batcha* to amuse them in their leisure hours. These boys receive as much attention as the most popular actress in other quarters of the globe, and experience in the same way the fickleness of public favour, for when they become too old for dancing, they find a difficulty in starting in any other line of life, the name *batcha* being often affixed as a sort of stigma, when their short reign of popularity is over. A favourite method with the patrons of the *batcha* is to set him up in a tea-shop, of which he can, if he is clever, make a great success. More often the *batcha* is spoilt and demoralized by the life and the attentions bestowed on him, takes to smoking opium or drinking *kukhuar*, and soon dies of dissipation. The dances are generally mere posturing accompanied by songs, or a kind of pantomime of the emotions; while others consist of gymnastic feats, somersaults, leaps and springs, and all to the music of tambourines and the measured clapping of the audience, who follow the movements spell-bound. The dancers are usually dressed in long silken robes, and in some of the most popular dances are attired as women, with long braids of false hair, tinkling anklets, and bracelets. Since the Russian conquest restrictions have been placed on these performances, and the number of dancers has decreased.

Besides dancers, there are comedians, such as are seen in India and other Eastern countries. These, with whitened faces (which remind one oddly of the pantomime clown so well known to Western playgoers), and a bit of rag or a few cloths to simulate various garbs, will act small comedies, often very obscene and vulgar, but undeniably clever; representations of familiar street scenes, buyer and seller, *Kazi* and suitor, teacher and scholar; or will mimic animals in an extremely life-like manner.

The festivals of saints, some of whom were merely successful warriors, with no particular claim to sanctity, are great opportunities for recreation, which usually takes the form of a pilgrimage to the tomb, and a kind of fair and picnic combined. Booths are erected, and the ground is covered with tents and little enclosures, in which music and dancing are largely patronized.

There are certain epochs in the life of a Mussulman in Central Asia which are also marked by feasting and merry-making. The ninth day after his birth must be observed with more or less ceremony, according to the means of his parents. The most elaborate feasts take place, however, when the boys are circumcised, which in Central Asia is usually between the ages of seven and ten. It is *de rigueur* at these times that the friends of the family should be invited, regaled with all the delicacies that can be procured, and afterwards entertained with music and dancing, so that the festival is an expensive one. Two or three men, having sons to be circumcised, frequently join together in giving a feast.

Among the Sarts—the dwellers in towns (practically the merchant and artisan classes of Central Asia)—a boy is considered marriageable from the age of fifteen or sixteen, and a girl between eleven and fifteen, or even earlier, although this is becoming rare. The courtship, as in all Mussulman countries, is carried on through a third person, who arranges the amount of *kalim*, or purchase-money, which is not always paid to the parents, as among more primitive tribes, but is a kind of marriage settlement. Before the marriage feasts are given by the bride to her friends, and by the bridegroom to his, and on the wedding-day a grand feast to all friends and relations is given in the bride's house. The marriage ceremony is performed by a *mullah*, or priest, but neither of the contracting parties is present, being represented by male relatives. The wedding presents are usually given by nines, that being the sacred number; and the guests not only bring, but receive, gifts. When the ceremony is over, the bridegroom can go to the women's court and claim his bride. Probably she will be concealed amidst a group of women, and he must find her hand before he can lead her out—no easy task, as he has most likely never seen her before!

The position of women in Mussulman countries can never be enviable, but in Central Asian towns she has certain rights, and if her husband does not provide for her in the way his means allow, or that by rank she is entitled to, she can complain to the *Kazi*, or judge, a native functionary who in many places has been allowed by the Russian conquerors to continue in his former position. The *Kazi*, if he think fit, can empower her to borrow money on her husband's account, or even sell his property to obtain what she wants. Divorce is, however, easy for the husband, who need give no reason, but must, if he parts with her, return to his wife all her belongings. She can also obtain a divorce if she can show good reason; and there is no obstacle to her remarriage unless her husband curses her, as he may if she has been guilty of any heinous crime.

The nomads naturally cannot afford the feasts which are the great indulgence and dissipation of the Sarts. Still, they have their own idea of amusements, and foremost among these are horse-racing and a game played on horseback called *Kok-bura*, or "grey wolf." The latter reminds one strongly of polo, if one can imagine polo played on a vast steppe, with sometimes as many as a hundred players. One man has a dead kid slung from his saddle-bow, and the object of the others is to bear away this kid and carry it safely to the judge. The skill of the Kirghiz in managing their horses, and the keen zest with which they enter into the game, make it very exciting and interesting to watch. As for horse-racing, it is a passion with all the nomads; and camel-racing is also popular, the ungainly beasts being sometimes driven by women or girls. The number of entries for a single horse-race got up at Orenburg not many years since was over a thousand. Rather a difficult post must be that of starter on a Central Asian racecourse!

The Russian Government does everything in its power to foster the breeding of horses—a very important matter in such a vast territory, where the maintenance of order is largely dependent upon irregular mounted troops. There are large studs for cavalry and artillery remounts in the

Orenburg district and Turkistan; but, indeed, wherever a Cossack is found, there will be horses. These hardy soldiers, themselves only second cousins to the Kirghiz whom they have subdued, are, like the nomads, born horsemen; but, unlike them, they take an interest in the improvement of their breed of horses. In Trans-Caucasia particularly there are many large private studs, and here the finest breeds are the Don, Kalmuk, and Kirghiz steppe horses, while elsewhere are found the Don Cossack and the two beautiful mountain breeds of Karabag and Kabardin. The Don Cossack, a most hardy and serviceable animal, is largely bred in the Governments of Orenburg and Ufa. Good agricultural horses are also bred here, and a draught horse of great power, known as the Bitygen, which shares with the camel and the huge Orenburg ox the whole inland trade between Russia and Asia at present. The steppe horses are all good for the saddle, more especially the Don, which, when improved with a strain of Arab or Persian, is noted above all Russian horses for lightness and speed, combined with endurance.

In Turkistan the two chief breeds are the Argamak and the Kirghiz, the former being of mixed breed, large and showy, and when well bred very expensive. Although a native of Central Asia, this horse has given his name to the Imperial stables at Moscow, which are still called the stables for the Argamaks—doubtless a reminiscence of the days of Mongol supremacy, when the Golden Horde dictated fashions to the Muscovite court. The Kirghiz is a much humbler animal, of no great speed, ugly and light in colour, and when in native hands is too often a victim to the passion of his master for *kumis* (soured mares' milk), which not only exhausts the mares, but prevents the foals from being well nourished. Nevertheless, the Kirghiz, living all the year round in the open air, is a hardy and useful horse, and remarkable for his retentive memory—an especially useful trait in the almost trackless steppes. As a light draught horse this animal does excellently, and will doubtless be largely used in Central Asian warfare in the future. A third breed, the Turkoman, is found in these parts; but it is seldom that a good one can be bought, so highly are they prized by their native owners. They are somewhat like Arabs in appearance, and are exceedingly reliable and hardy. The Kalmuk is an ugly horse, small, rough, and long-eared, but hardy and serviceable for light cavalry.

The Karabag, a native of the mountain regions of Turkistan, holds the same rank among Asiatic horses as the English thoroughbred among European, and is a most beautiful, elegant animal, with marvellously sure foot, very faithful and docile. The Kabardin is a mixture of Arab and mountain horse, and is not quite so fine and graceful as the Karabag, but has more endurance, and is both strong and fiery.

Travelling in Central Asia is usually accomplished either on horseback or in a cart resembling the Russian *taratass*, and is neither comfortable nor speedy unless good animals have been procured. The Russian post-roads in Central Asia are not level *chaussées*, but merely show the direction of the track, which is marked out by post relays, and a few settlements and towns. The posting-stations are generally kept by a rich Cossack, who manages this in addition to farming and keeping an inn. He has to provide by contract a certain number of post-horses and *telegas*. The postal communications are under the control of a *smoitritel*, usually an old soldier who examines all the passports, and has also to see to the replenishing of the inevitable *samovar*, getting a few copecks for his trouble. The station has a bare whitewashed room for the convenience of travellers, containing little furniture but a table, some wooden stools, and the tea apparatus. Sometimes the posting-station is only a Kirghiz tent, and in past days not unfrequently consisted of nothing but a water-cask and a post besmeared with the Russian colours. The *telega*, or posting-car, is a small open wooden cart scarcely five feet in length, resting on four small wooden wheels, and running on two wooden axles. In the steppes the wheels frequently have neither metal rims nor boxes, so that the axles catch fire in spite of being perpetually greased. A feather and a jar of grease are an essential part of a traveller's equipment, and he must personally and at short intervals superintend the greasing if he wishes to avoid a breakdown and the serious consequences. On the front box of the *telega* the coachman, or *jemschtchik*, is perched, and the traveller must make a seat of a bundle of straw, or his bag lashed to the cart. To this he must stick as closely as he can, while the Cossack horses gallop madly with the *telega*, which is innocent of springs, across the trackless steppe, over streams and hills and trunks of trees. The traveller after a few days of this sort of journey is almost deprived of feeling, indeed of any sensation, and those unaccustomed to it require some time to recover. Yet the couriers, who carry important despatches, travel so night and day for several days, only waiting at each posting-station for tea, while fresh horses are brought. Innumerable glasses of tea, a few biscuits and eggs, frequently form their diet on the journey, and sometimes not even this. The difficulty of transporting troops and arms in such a country and for such distances may readily be imagined, and it is marvellous to think that Tamerlane traversed these deserts with a million men. Modern armies, with their elaborate organization,—especially intricate commissariat and ambulance—can never accomplish what has been done in the past on many occasions by hordes of nomad horsemen; subsisting like the hardy animals that carried them on what they could pick up on the almost barren steppe—roots, dried meat, or a bird shot and hastily cooked.

A common and picturesque sight is a caravan

starting, let us say, from Orenburg. The long snake-like procession of waggons is drawn by the powerful Russian ox, or the gigantic Asiatic buffalo, and winds slowly across the steppes, the ungreased wooden wheels creaking and groaning, the Cossack coachman calling every now and then to his team from his seat in a kennel of straw erected at the top of a bale of goods. Halting before a Cossack *stanitza*, they form the waggons into a sort of little fortified camp or laager; and as we rattle by in our *telega* we see the light of the camp fire, round which the weary drivers bivouac until the dawn, just like Boers on the trek.

One of the most characteristic features of life in all parts of Central Asia is the custom of present giving, which has attained proportions undreamt of in western lands, though even there it is still an important factor in social life. Presents in Central Asia are by no means voluntary or spontaneous, being given and received as a matter of course, and it is not customary to return thanks for gifts until one is congratulated on receiving them, when thanks must be returned—not for the gift, but for the congratulations. They would become a serious tax were it not that whoever receives a present must promptly give one in return. Among the Kirghiz (who carry the custom to great lengths, despite the fact that their only wealth consists practically of the tent they live in and their flocks), etiquette demands, for instance, that at a funeral feast every mourner who attends must receive a present; but then he must always bring one with him, and the two must be of equal value, so that the proprieties are satisfied, and no one is either loser or gainer in this game of forfeits. Amusing stories are told of gifts sent to each other by the rulers of the various Khanates, in pre-Russian days, which eventually found their way back to the original sender; and one is reminded of the lady who settled in Germany, and found some difficulty in thinking of a suitable gift for the birthday of a friend, which according to the custom of the country could by no means be neglected. Finally she sent a brass candlestick, which was greeted with effusion, and followed on her own birthday by the gift of a matchbox. Next year the problem again presented itself, and in some trepidation she packed up the matchbox and sent it to join the candlestick. A letter of most effusive thanks was again received, and on her birthday—the candlestick returned intact! Now, it is said, they exchange matchbox and candlestick every year, plus two letters of polite and "heart-warmest greetings." This system, very closely followed in Central Asia, is a great nuisance to a stranger, who, wishing to join at all in social life, is confronted at the outset by what seems an overwhelming tax on his resources and ingenuity. A native who offers the smallest civility or present—a bunch of grapes or flowers—will remark, as he does so, "*Sillau keryak*"—a present is necessary.

All over Central Asia we find traces of a civilization so old that it has been entirely forgotten, and nothing remains to tell us what were the races who dwelt there, or how they fell from their high estate. On the north bank of the Syr Daria, all along the valley, are numerous ruins which mark the sites of former cities; and legend says that this district, now a wilderness with an occasional Russian fort or small half-savage town, was once so densely populated that from Kashgar to the Sea of Aral "the nightingale could fly from branch to branch, and the cat walk from house-top to house-top." No investigations have as yet given a clue as to the identity of the once busy dwellers in this fertile valley, nor why their towns fell into decay. The country is quite capable of supporting a population; in summer, plants and flowers of many varieties bloom on the steppes, and the brush which grows on the river banks forms a cover for quantities of pheasants, geese, partridges, and other game.

Perhaps the most interesting and mysterious of these relics of bygone ages are found in the country around Lake Issyk-Kul, and on the banks of that lake itself. Here, no doubt, in ancient times were several cities, and under water there are ruins visible, which make it appear likely that the lake has risen, or else that there has been a subsidence of the soil. Very curious relics are washed up—large tiles and bricks, covered with red and blue glaze, broken pottery, human bones, and metallic vessels. A traveller in 1876 was shown a lamp with an inscription on it in an entirely unknown language. Chinese maps of an early period place a city named Tchi-gu on the shores of Issyk-Kul, and on the Catalan map of 1375 there is marked on the southern shore a Nestorian monastery containing the bones of St. Matthew. The great route which runs through Central Asia from east to west passes between Lake Issyk-Kul and Tashkent, through ground of classic, or one might almost say pre-classic memory. On one of the mountains which lie south of the little country town of Aulie-ata, legend has it that Noah's ark rested after the subsidence of the deluge; and the fact that this is told of at least half a dozen other mountains in Asia does not prevent a certain number of believers from visiting it to behold the remains which are still to be seen. This, too, was undoubtedly the country of Prester John, that mysterious Napoleon of the Middle Ages, who has been identified with a successful Khan and conqueror known as Yeliu Tashi. His capital, Bala Sagun, the chief city of the Karikidans, has vanished completely; but perhaps one day, when the buried cities of Asia are properly investigated, and railways run from one "interesting ruin" to another for the benefit of tourists, the capital of Prester John may be discovered, buried in the sand, and we may yet learn the rights of the marvellous story of the Christian pagan, half pope, half king, who loomed so large on the imagination of mediæval times.

Over this road passed the earliest traveller whose records remain to us—Zemarchus, an ambassador from the Emperor Justinian in 569, who was sent to visit Dizabulus, probably Dalobian Khan, a powerful chief living on the northern slope of the Thian Shan. The next traveller came from the east, sixty years later, in the person of Hiuen Tsiang, a Buddhist pilgrim and student. He peoples the mountains and Lake Issyk-Kul with terrible monsters and dragons, but describes enthusiastically a lovely valley, "the place of a thousand springs," where the Turkish Khan had his summer residence, and where beautiful woods were full of tame stags all adorned with bells and rings. This spot is probably the triangle formed by the river Tchu and its tributary, the Kurgati.

Nearly all the tribes who, until the Russian era, possessed the soil in Central Asia, date themselves back to Genghiz Khan; but an account of his conquests, given by a Chinese statesman who accompanied that warrior during his progress West, in the early years of the thirteenth century, gives a description of towns which existed then and are still standing, such as Hodjent, Samarkand, and Bokhara. It is almost certain that Central Asia was never under a homogeneous rule. Genghiz Khan, sweeping from east to west, gathered up all the little tribes, and destroyed many ancient kingdoms; but he immediately divided his immense territories between his sons, and they, when their turn came, did likewise, so that the family of Genghiz became a sort of hereditary aristocracy over the whole of Central Asia. Thus, among Kirghiz, Kara-Kirghiz, Kalmuks, Uzbeks, and all tribes which have any of the Mongol element, the "white bones" still love to boast of their descent from the great conqueror.

In the twelfth century two other Chinese travellers also braved the perils of the route through Central Asia, and both describe the country of the "Karakitai" as full of ancient ruins. In 1253 we have an account of a missionary journey, undertaken by Rubruquis, a Flemish friar, at the instigation of St. Louis of France. He found the Nestorians already established, but notes that in many of the cities the people worship idols, while others are entirely Mohammedan. He also mentions with surprise a little village, which was inhabited by "Saracens, speaking Persian, though such a huge way from Persia," just as the Tadjik of our own day speaks an Aryan dialect with words of Persian derivation which have dropped out of use in their native land. The most imaginative traveller, however, was King Hethum of Cis, in Cilicia, a Christian monarch who went to visit Mangu Khan. His account of the "Kingdom of Dogs" has been referred to in the description of the Kirghiz.

One of the Chinese travellers already alluded to notices a city near Aulie-ata, the remains of which are still to be seen, and are among the most curious ruins in the world. Native legend says that this city was built by a prince of the Divs, or mountain spirits, who fell in love with a maiden who lived near, and wishing to build a city for her to live in, threw down great stones from his mountain. These ruins are thirty miles east of Aulie-ata, and their extent, and the size of the stones used to build them, excuse some stretch of the imagination in order to account for their presence. An immense unfinished building, 600 feet by 450, is built of reddish sandstone, some stones used in the lower layers being seven feet long by four broad. Lerch, who investigated the ruins, thinks they may have been intended for a Buddhist monastery. The same traveller mentions certain great grave mounds which stand to this day, silent but eloquent witnesses to the transience of human fame; for doubtless the long-forgotten race who built them meant them as an enduring monument to some national heroes, whose memory they hoped would thus be immortalized.

When one considers the numbers of races which have met, amalgamated, or in many cases simply settled down side by side in Central Asia, one cannot be surprised at a certain amount of confusion in their method of reckoning time. Simplest of all, the Kirghiz, having no era from which to date their years, use a twelve-year cycle, and give to each cycle the name of an animal, the names being arranged in a certain sequence. The day of the year is not regarded at all, every one born in the same year being considered as of the same age. The Kirghiz day is divided into four parts—sunrise, eating-time, midday, and sunset. Seven days make a week, or *atna*, while the year is divided into twelve solar months, bearing names corresponding to the signs of the zodiac in Arabic. These Arabic names were translated from the Greek, and the Greek names, say Assyriologists, were originally borrowed directly, or through Egypt, from those given to the months by the Chaldean and Babylonian astronomers. These were not connected with agricultural occupations, but with the periodic changes in the heavenly bodies, to each of which names had been given which had become part of the mythology of the people. The deities thus evolved were embodied in emblematic figures, and these figures remain much the same to this day—Virgo, for instance, having originally represented the Goddess Ishtar; while some of the signs have lost their original meaning, and are improvements on the earliest signs, such as Aquarius, which is an amplification of the water-pail, and so forth. These names, which describe the different periods of the solar year, must have been introduced into Central Asia at a very remote period, and are still in use there in their original form. This calendar is far more complete and sensible than that now being introduced by Russia—the Julian, which is already more than twelve days out of its reckoning. Besides these zodiacal names, the Kirghiz, like all simple people, have given titles to the months descriptive of their occupations at different times of the year; and, much as the English labourer talks of sowing-time, harvest, and hay-harvest, the nomad speaks of lambing-time, mare-milking season, and the slaughtering season. The Kirghiz are well acquainted with the stars, by which they steer their path in the desert, as well as using them to calculate time. The same solar year, with twelve months named after the zodiacal signs, is in use among all agriculturists, the months having in Tashkent alternately thirty and thirty-one days, while the last month has in ordinary years only twenty-nine, with an extra day every four years. In other cities another system is adopted, rather less regular, and containing one month of thirty-two days and two of twenty-nine—a method common to agriculturists in Persia as well as Central Asia, and in the former country also used by Government in the assessment of taxes. A rhyme, resembling our own "Thirty days hath September," is commonly used in both countries to keep the different days of the month in the memory. There is also the ordinary Mussulman calendar, consisting of a lunar year, used in all religious documents and by the educated classes generally; and since the Julian calendar has been introduced by the Russians, great confusion has inevitably ensued.

CHAPTER VI

THE BRITISH RULE IN INDIA

THERE is little room for doubt that, with a wise policy which must at once be bold and resolute, while India herself remains contented and loyal, Britain has little to fear in her Eastern Empire from foreign aggression. So long as she can thoroughly depend upon the support of both the native agricultural masses and military element, she is strong for defence. So much being granted, it would seem a politic measure to discover, as far as possible, to what extent she *can* rely upon such support. Statistics as to the prosperity or progress of the country are no doubt valuable enough in their way; but, in order to arrive at anything like an accurate conclusion as to the internal strength of Britain's Indian Empire, it is necessary to investigate beyond these, and to find out what is the prevailing feeling amongst the natives towards their rulers, both local and imperial.

Is India so governed as to ensure the contentment and, should circumstances so require, the loyal support of her people? Unpleasant though the truth may be, the answer to this question is, to say the least, problematical. The entire population of the country amounts to about three hundred millions, two hundred and fifty millions of whom are agriculturists, who "scratch the soil, harvest the crops, and pay heavy taxes." Of the remaining fifty millions, a proportion of from one-half to two-thirds are fighting men, settled principally in the Punjaub, but also to be found in Rajputana, Oudh, and other provinces. The people are far from homogeneous, as shown later, and are of different creeds as well as races. In the administration of such a mighty empire, England has no easy task to perform. Her system of government may be—and probably is, all things considered—a better one than the natives could hope for under any other rule; but, even so, there is much that needs reform. And without question one of the first reforms should be to give to the British rule in India less of a machine-like aspect, and to introduce more of the personal element. At present the people are unknown to their rulers and the rulers to the people. It has been aptly remarked that before the Mutiny "the people had rulers; now they have only rules." The majority of the officials, mixing almost exclusively as they do with their English colleagues, and finding the greater part of their time fully occupied in transacting the vast amount of detailed work connected with their respective departments, have little opportunity for acquiring an intimate knowledge of, or a practical sympathy with, the native population; and should any one of them, indeed, attempt to introduce a reform, he receives but small encouragement from the Indian or the Home authorities. Reformers are even less popular in India than elsewhere.

The Central Government and high officials live, in fact, in a world of their own, and will not hear of any such thing as discontent—still less that it can be due to the best possible system in the best of worlds. None the less is the evil at work, and to a dangerous extent. The tendency in India is increasingly towards bureaucracy of a hard-and-fast type. The avenue to a career or rapid promotion in India is through the portals of the Secretariat—the official "Holy of Holies;" and the governments are composed of men who, endowed with industry, a ready pen, and the art of report-writing, have yet never been outside the walls of the Secretariats in Calcutta and Simla. Such men know little more of the native of India—his aspirations, his hopes, his fears—than might an average permanent official in Downing Street. The "paper-rule" system of India—an impersonal one—has grown to such an extent that it is a grave danger. From the poor peasant in his field to the Secretary of State for India—through all the successive stages of district officer, provincial administration, and the Government of India—is a far cry. *Laissez faire* and *Surtout pas trop de zèle* are the watchwords of this highest form yet known in the evolution of Circumlocution.

In the place of laws issued by a far-distant Government, and administered by unknown and unsympathetic officials, the people want a more *personal* rule: they want judgments they can follow and understand. Justice, at the price which they now have to pay for it, is beyond their means, and so it comes about that the poor, who constitute the vast majority of the population, are oppressed, while the wealthy classes flourish. There can be little doubt that to continue to force on the people a code of laws suitable only to Western civilization, or to attempt the introduction of democratic government, would be at the present time, whatever it may be in the future, a vast mistake. In reality, India consists of an assemblage of nations of different interests, languages, and creeds—a congregation of races and tribes in no sense of the word homogeneous, who are, in fact, antagonistic, and the vast majority of whom are but little higher in the scale of humanity than the natives of Africa. Radical differences exist among the numerous tribes with regard to caste, intelligence, and many other characteristics, rendering the advent of Western ideals for many generations to come an impossibility.

The chief difference is, of course, in the fighting quality, which varies in a peculiar degree and differentiates the various races. Speaking generally, the Mohammedan is warlike, the Hindu is not; the one is masterful and courageous, the other supple and craven; the one represents force, the other words—points which should never be lost sight of.

"The strong, fierce, independent warrior of the north," says Sir Lepel Griffin, "has a deep-rooted contempt for the smooth, subtle, and cowardly lowlander, who is neither fit to fight or to govern, but who is his superior in the art of intrigue, who can beat him in every competitive competition, and to whom will fall the whole weight of any political concessions that agitation can wring from the timidity of the Government. The world is ruled by strength and courage, and not by competitive examinations."

Once we lose sight of this truth, we may prepare for the "barbarians from the north, who cannot read or write, but who seal their treaties with the pommel of the sword." The backbone of the Indian army is supplied by the Sikhs and Rajputs, who are unsurpassed as soldiers, and whose courage and devotion have been tested on many battle-fields and in many lands. Led by British officers, they are probably superior to *ordinary* Russian troops. To give power to the Bengalis, troublesome in time of peace and useless in time of war—as would surely be the effect of a further development of democratic government, with its representative institutions —would be to alienate the Sikhs and Rajputs, with whom the Bengalis have absolutely nothing in common. In fact, the doctrine of equality, as preached in the West, is totally inapplicable to India at the present time.

What is required is a simpler law with a less complex administration. Western law has been introduced into—indeed, forced upon—this Oriental land, without due regard for the customs and sentiments of its many millions of poverty-stricken people. What is suitable for highly educated Europe, with its complex society, is quite unsuited for these toiling and moiling millions, who simply want "to fill their bellies, pay their taxes, and meet the interest due on their debts."

"In England," says Thorburn, "a lawsuit is a costly luxury, indulged in by the rich and quarrelsome alone; in India it is, owing to over-government, a necessity for all classes, a debt-collecting instrument for creditors, and the only means open to agriculturists for the settlement of their generally simple disputes *inter se.* It has no terrors for the mercantile and money-lending classes. They have money at command, education, and subtle intelligences, which delight in the intricacy and surprises of a good case in court. But for the peasant, artisan, or village menial, who form the bulk of the peoples of India, it often means ruin." *

* S. S. Thorburn, "Asiatic Neighbours."

Such being the state of affairs, it is little wonder that discontent is on the increase, and that the natives are becoming less trustful, less confident in England's strength—a state of mind which is ready to accept the growing belief in the power of the great Northern Colossus that aspires to dominate Asia.

Another unfortunate feature, and this closely affecting the whole social life of the people, is to be found in the widespread influence of the Hindu money-lending class, an influence which is especially dominant in the Punjaub, where many of the old village communities have been replaced by the "rule of usurers." Since the time of the Mutiny a large proportion of the cultivated land in this district—a proportion estimated, indeed, at ten per cent. for some localities and even twenty-five for others—has been wrested from the peasantry by the money-lenders, who are gradually but surely undermining the prosperity of the agricultural population, the latter being always ready to blame the Government for their misfortunes in this direction. The farmers, and the peasantry generally, borrow money in order to pay their debts and to avoid lawsuits of any description, knowing well that their chances of success against a wealthy opponent, who can afford to employ a clever lawyer, are but small. If they do find themselves in the courts, they have to borrow money for their defence, with the natural consequence that the money-lender, who charges a high rate of interest, in the end becomes possessed of the borrowers' land. In this way a large proportion of the cultivated land has passed into the hands of the usurers, the peasantry becoming tenants instead of proprietors, being eventually, perhaps, evicted; and it goes without saying that such a state of affairs gives rise to much discontent and bad feeling, the blame being laid, as has been said, on the method of civil administration favoured by the Indian Government. It is only to be expected that the peasantry will eventually become incensed at their ever-increasing impoverishment, and that they will be ready to take advantage of any opportunity that offers to emancipate themselves. Probably they would long ago have made a stand for their rights, were it not that they occasionally receive the sympathy of the local English officials, who do what they can to render the law less oppressive; whilst another reason for their patient endurance may be found in the fact that they still cherish a hope that Government intervention will come to their aid. There is no doubt that this is essentially a matter to be dealt with by the Indian Government itself. That reform of some sort is urgently needed is a self-evident fact, and, as a simple act of justice, as well as a measure of policy, it should no longer be delayed.

The present condition of affairs undoubtedly renders the struggle for existence a hard one, as may be realized when it is considered that a vast population of about three hundred millions, distributed in the proportion of between 500 and 800 to the square mile of cultivated land, suffers not only from the inevitable droughts which so frequently occur, but also from a narrow and short-sighted Imperial policy, which places every obstacle in the way of industrial development, and imposes heavy taxes on the struggling people. With the peasantry as a whole, and especially those on the north-western frontiers, discontented and dissatisfied with their present rulers, a most favourable opportunity is presented to Russia to make her influence felt, and, later on, when she has been able to approach still nearer to the frontier, to ensure to herself a welcome. She might even, as she herself anticipates, be greeted as a "deliverer." And, indeed, according to various authorities, her demands upon landowners in her Central Asian possessions are not so exacting as are ours in India, for the British Government insists on a fifth of the produce, making no allowance for good or bad years; while Russia is said to ask only a tenth, and to allow for variations of production.

Only if some reform is made in the abuses noted can Britain hope to preserve, under all circumstances, the loyalty of her Indian subjects. Meanwhile, all assurances regarding the loyalty of the native princes and people, and of the enthusiasm for British rule, must be received with extreme reserve. By what ties are they bound to their masters? Not those of blood, or creed, or common aims and aspirations; merely that of self-interest, which will side with the British so long as they are strong, and so long as there is no cause for discontent. The loyalty of a hungry and over-taxed people to an alien, a distant and impersonal power, cannot be relied upon. And, in any case, let it never be forgotten that the British element in the Indian army is the keystone of all loyalty, for it is that of strength.

It must not, however, be assumed that the money-lenders are solely to blame for the poverty and the generally reduced status of the agricultural population. Another fruitful cause is the over-taxation which is prevalent. The manner in which, for instance, the Punjaub peasantry are "squeezed" in order to counterbalance the loss of revenue in Bengal consequent upon the "Permanent Settlement" effected by Lord Cornwallis in 1793, is a source of discontent amongst a brave and hardy population whose value to England from a military point of view, in the event of invasion, cannot be overestimated.

By the "Cornwallis Settlement" it was arranged that the farmers and others holding land under the then current decennial settlement should become the "landlords" of such "estates" for ever, on condition of paying to the State the assessments then in force. This arrangement, carried out without survey or investigation of titles, was of course most advantageous to the farmers who happened to hold land in 1793; but the result has been the loss of fabulous amounts to the Imperial exchequer, and the creation of a dangerous degree of discontent amongst the peasantry, upon whom a consequently higher taxation than would otherwise be the case is forced.

The danger from over-taxation is indeed extreme. India is poor and cannot bear the burden.* She is gradually being pushed towards a state of insolvency. Protests have on various occasions been made against the taxation of such necessary articles as salt, etc. Much ill-feeling has also been from time to time aroused in connection with the cotton duties, which have been enforced or abolished without any consideration of the prosperity or otherwise that might be entailed thereby, the sole object, in every case, being to forward the interests of the Lancashire operatives, whose votes are required. It is well to emphasize the fact that it is far from an unusual proceeding on the part of Britain to subordinate the interests of her great dependency to party motives—a mistaken policy

* "I do not hesitate to say that half our agricultural population never know from year's end to year's end what it is to have their hunger satisfied" (Sir Charles Elliott, late Member of the Viceroy's Council, and Lieutenant-Governor of Bengal).

which hastens India towards insolvency, and can only have the effect of weakening her rule in her Eastern Empire. That, in order to secure a few votes, some feeble Ministry should, to conciliate sectional interest or philanthropic faddists, allow the imposition on India of measures disastrous both to her exchequer and to her people, is not likely to be productive of good feeling between rulers and ruled, and warnings on this point have not been absent.

Such matters are quickly seized upon as subject for agitation, against both the Indian and Imperial Governments, by the army of sedition-mongers who have sprung into existence as a consequence of the practically free education offered to all classes in India.

And in this connection it may be said that education is, in many respects, well carried out. The State itself provides for the teaching of all elementary subjects, and village schools are numerous. The higher education is, to a large extent, carried out by means of municipal or private benevolence; but Government grants are made to such schools as are willing to adopt Government methods, and to permit inspection and examination. The agricultural population have not, on the whole, taken advantage of their privileges to the extent which might have been expected, and therefore it is the town-dwellers who have benefited most largely. There is still much to be desired.

> "Education on English lines," says Thorburn, "carried out in India imparts learning of a sort without principle, makes a Bengali into a prig, a Mohammedan into a poor imitation of a vicious Englishman, an up-country Hindu into a selfish agnostic, and all who fail to make money or get Government service into grievance-mongers. An English boy starts in life with the moral force called principle ingrown in him: an Indian student—after cramming moral text-books for years—with nothing developed in him but self-seeking. Half the former's education is from his healthy home and school surroundings. Of these the latter can know nothing."

Introduced into the country with the best intentions, these educational advantages have by no means invariably produced happy results, for, as has been said, they have given rise to the existence of an immense number of superficially educated men who, finding the supply of lucrative posts inadequate, are either unable to secure employment or have been forced to accept almost nominal salaries, and, thus disappointed in their ambition, have turned their attention and energies to agitating against the Government, and generally to the promotion of sedition.

In order to arrive at some clear idea of Britain's true position in India, one of the points requiring careful consideration is her policy with regard to the hill-tribes, and her administration generally on the north-western frontiers. These tribes fall naturally into four divisions: (1) those between Peshawur and the Gilgit Agency, (2) those inhabiting the mountainous country between the Khyber pass and the Kurram valley, (3) the Waziri and other tribes found in the Suliman mountains, (4) those in Beluchistan controlled by the British agent. The inhabitants of the deserts and hills of Beluchistan are said to be of Arab descent, and were formerly merely marauding nomads. At one time their occupation of the Punjaub and Sindh was imminent, but they were overcome by force of British arms. These tribes, devoted to their chiefs, are more difficult to deal with than the Afghans, who can generally be bought, and who are always amenable to superior force. Much money has already been expended in the country for the purpose of securing British interests. In the earlier days of the British occupation, and even after the Sikhs themselves had been finally conquered, lawlessness in the north-western districts was rampant. The hill-tribes continually made raids into the lowlands, plundering the villages, seizing the cattle, and even killing the inhabitants. Gradually, however, order was to some extent introduced, the task being entrusted to selected officers to whom an exceedingly free hand in the matter was allowed. And, indeed, by reason of the vast distances separating them from the central authorities, it would have been practically impossible for the latter to exercise effective control. Various were the methods resorted to for the establishment of a system of security for property and life. Amongst some of the tribes the leading natives were dealt with, and power and authority given to them over their own districts. This system, however, did not always produce satisfactory results, for these native leaders discovered that, by exciting the tribes to the point of revolt, and then taking credit for pacifying them, they frequently could secure increase of salary and other benefits from the Government.

A more successful method was that of converting many of the hill-men into frontier police, and by giving them a fixed salary, doing away with all inducement to marauding expeditions. As in China, the system of communal responsibility was adopted in order to insure the detection and punishment of offenders; that is to say, when any offence was committed, the whole village or tribe, as the case might be, to which the offender belonged, was held responsible until the evil-doer was handed over to the authorities for punishment; failing his production, a fine was levied on the community concerned. This system was not altogether pleasing to the hill-tribes, and consequently gave rise to frequent disturbances amongst the more turbulent, occasionally even resulting in a declaration of war against the Government by some more than usually aggrieved tribe. To quell these risings expeditions were sent, at great expense, to the field of action, the whole affair being perhaps eventually settled, without much loss on either side, by the exaction of a nominal fine. These expeditions, in fact, were frequently awaited by the tribes with a feeling rather of expectation than of dread, for the natives had already learnt that an extremely humane policy towards them was to be relied upon; and the introduction of so many troops into a district brought with it opportunities for trading and other benefits. Matters assumed a different aspect, however, when the Snider breech-loader was introduced amongst the troops of the native army, for the hill-men found that their antiquated matchlocks were of very little use in opposing such weapons. So great, indeed, was their admiration for the new breech-loader rifle that the Government troops found the greatest difficulty in preserving their weapons against theft.

Hitherto no Government has been able to effectively tame the trans-frontier tribes, and, even after fifty years of endeavour and lavish expenditure, Britain has succeeded only in establishing her influence over certain of the Afridis, a small number of the Baluchis, and a few others. Such a result would seem to augur ill for the success of any British scheme to conciliate or subdue the remaining wild and independent tribes existing in Afghanistan and on its borders. But it is open to question whether the leniency exercised by the various punitive expeditions which have from time to time been sent against the border tribes has been the wisest course to pursue. These turbulent and warlike people learn no lesson from a mere exhibition of strength, and it is possible that a rigorous and decisive assertion of authority would be a quicker, cheaper, and in every way more effective mode of enforcing order.

In late years the whole system of frontier administration has been improved and strengthened, the law being adapted as far as possible to the requirements of the people, whilst direct communication between tribal leaders and the British officials has been encouraged, with satisfactory results. Communications have been developed, and strategic railways constructed, rendering a concentration of troops at any given point a comparatively easy matter; whilst Quetta and New Chaman, within 400 miles of Kandahar, have been connected by rail with the frontier, and roads have been rendered practicable for vehicular traffic. The expenditure necessitated by this vigorous policy has naturally been large, but the advantages obtained cannot be over-estimated. The tribesmen are beginning to see where their true interests lie, and are devoting themselves, though slowly, to peaceful pursuits, to the benefit, not only of themselves, but of the Empire at large.

With regard to the tribes beyond our actual border, who may yet be considered practically under British control, it is a significant fact that, even to the present day, little progress has been made in turning them from their wild and lawless condition. Expeditions have been from time to time sent into the little explored country which they inhabit, but with little result. Owing to the mountainous and generally difficult nature of the country, many of these tribes live in a state of isolation so far as the outer world is concerned; their power for offence is small, for their weapons are crude and antiquated, but, as in the case of South Africa, the impregnable nature of the mountain fastnesses would render the task of subduing these clans a costly affair, and one necessitating the expenditure of much time and many lives. Most of these frontier tribes are priest-ridden, but the introduction of British authority generally produces a change in this respect. One of the most turbulent of the trans-frontier populations is the Mohmand tribe, which has on more than one occasion caused trouble. In the Afghan war of 1880 they even attempted to block the Khyber pass, but were quickly dispersed by the British troops. The Afridis, in the neighbourhood of the Kohat district, are another powerful fighting race, many of whom have in recent years enlisted in the native Indian army, and have from time to time rendered effective assistance to the British, notably during the Mutiny. The Khyber and Kohat passes are both under the domination of this tribe, and Government annually pays them a large sum in order that travellers shall not be interfered with.

The area occupied by all these independent trans-frontier tribes includes many thousands of square miles, and their total number amounts to something like a million, of whom a fifth may be regarded as fighting men. The task of converting them into orderly and friendly neighbours is a gigantic one, and would seem almost impossible of achievement, for these Pathans are an obstinate and fanatical people, on whom, as a rule, nothing has any influence but force. Nevertheless, the Indian Government has set itself to the task, and, though it may necessitate time, patience, and serious expense, it is evident that whatever measure of success is attained is a step in the right direction.

Taking a general survey of the situation, it would appear that there are dangers threatening Britain in India, not merely from without, but also from within: dangers arising from over-government, and an attempt to prematurely force on the country Western ideas and institutions; the sacrificing of Indian interests to party considerations in England; unwise or impolitic administration generally, as exemplified in the tolerance of money-lending extortions, interference with native customs, and unjust taxation,—all these breeding discontent and alienating the loyalty of our best friends, who are the fighting men of the Punjaub.

The present policy of defence, merely guarding the passes which debouch on the plains next the Indus—altogether insufficient for the defence of the Empire, as will be shown later on—is making increasing demands upon the financial resources of the country, demands which are difficult to satisfy. The closer approach of a great military Power like Russia—especially when in command of important strategic positions in Afghanistan—will entail upon India "such an intolerable amount of expense, in the shape of additional fortifications and other measures of defence, as would become absolutely intolerable, and would be less preferable than any other alternative, however serious." *

It is to be hoped that the necessary internal reforms will be carried out, and the measures needed for effective defence of the Empire, indicated later on, will be boldly undertaken. Britain must share the cost of defending India, for on the security of her Eastern dominions depends the stability of the British world-empire. Only then will India be secure from internal disaffection, and unassailable by any hostile foreign influence from without.

* The Marquis of Dufferin and Ava.

CHAPTER VII

AFGHANISTAN AND PERSIA

It is now necessary to consider the parts likely to be played by Afghanistan and Persia respectively in the fateful world-drama now being enacted in Central Asia—a drama whose further development holds such momentous possibilities for the whole of Europe and the United States, but especially for Great Britain.

The Indo-Russian question sprang into existence in 1800, when, as already said, Napoleon and Paul contemplated the conquest of India by the ancient route of invasion, one followed from Alexander to Nadir Shah. Briefly stated the British policy has been, by various means, to retard the advance of Russia towards India, to use Afghanistan as a buffer and thus create an efficient Indian frontier defence. Towards this end we have had wars with Persia and Afghanistan, and diplomacy has been applied to Central

Asia, with no success. The present Amir is our subsidized ally; but his term of life is uncertain, and his people still remain the unruly, fickle, treacherous, independence-loving people they ever were. With the Amir's death there will be anarchy, inviting the intervention of Russia and England, and perhaps other Powers.

The two Afghan wars of 1838–42 and 1878–80 cost Britain over forty-five millions sterling, the expenditure on other wars beyond the Indus bringing the total up to seventy millions. The calamitous first Afghan campaign, the Sikh and Crimean wars, the Sind and Punjaub annexations, and the Sepoy Mutiny, made any forward movement of England in Afghanistan impossible for many years. After the suppression of the Mutiny, Russia, then sufficiently recovered from the Crimean war, was allowed unopposed to pursue her advance in Central Asia. Within the years 1860–68 she had advanced her frontiers to the neighbourhood of Afghanistan, and with insignificant expenditure of men and money. Afghanistan, now become the sole territory lying between the two great Asiatic Powers, was in a state of grave disorder, weak, and impotent. She became the buffer between Russia and India. Two British schools arose, termed respectively "mischievous activity" and "masterly inactivity," of which the most able exponents were Sir Henry Rawlinson and Mr. Wyllie, of the Indian Foreign Office, the latter expressing the views of the great Indian Viceroy, Sir John Lawrence. The former, a statesman in the best sense of the word, a diplomatist and man of action, showed clearly the dangers involved by the Russian advance, and laid special stress on the danger attaching to a Russian occupation of Herat; the latter ridiculed the "phantom of a Russian invasion."

"The panic-mongers of the press," wrote Wyllie, "military men, whose professional instincts lead them to sniff the battle afar off, and to mistrust our existing frontier line, whether along the Indus or at the foot of the Khaibar and Bolan passes beyond that river, as false to the principles of the art of war,—these are they who, to prove the possibility of invasion, cite the conquests of the Macedonian Alexander, of Timur, and of Nadir Shah, and who, in the so-called will of Peter the Great, the traditional policy of his successors, the treaty with Napoleon at Tilsit, and the immense development southward which the Siberian boundary has undoubtedly received, find cumulative evidence of Russia's determination to make the possibility an accomplished fact. According to these alarmists, what we have to expect is as follows: In a very short time the Russians will have military colonies on the Oxus, at Charjui and Takhtapul. From Charjui troops will be thrown across the desert to Merv, and from Merv the fertile banks of the Murgab offer easy access to Herat. Simultaneously, a smaller column will proceed through Takhtapul and the defiles of the Hindu Kush to occupy Kabul. Persia, of course, will act in alliance with the invaders, and at Herat the force from Charjui will be joined by large Russo-Persian reinforcements marching in from the shores of the Caspian Sea and the districts of Khorasan. Some delay must occur at Herat, for that city, the key of the position, will have to be fortified and provisioned, and a chain of smaller forts on either side will have to be established, stretching as far as Takhtapul in the north and Lake Seistan in the south. But the interval will bo well redeemed by disarming the hostility and securing the co-operation of the Afghans. The darling dream of the whole nation is to plunder India, and Russia will offer them that guerdon, and the restoration of their old provinces of Peshawar and Kashmir to boot. Then some fine morning early in spring . . . 40,000 disciplined troops of Russia and Persia, in conjunction with a countless horde of wild Afghan auxiliaries, will be launched, resistless as an avalanche, upon the doomed plains of the southern El Dorado, and there at once is the end of our Eastern empire."

"Politicians of another and far higher stamp," wrote Wyllie, in reply to the views of Rawlinson, as chief opponent of the "no-advance" school, "while they see clearly that any immediate or approximate danger of a Russian invasion is chimerical, nevertheless look forward with uneasiness to the inevitable day when the Russian and English Empires shall be conterminous, and the presence of a first-class European State on our border shall have the power at any time to fan into a flame those elements of sporadic disaffection which, of necessity, are ever smouldering in any country won and held, as India was and is, by an alien sword. For political reasons of obvious weight, they believe that it would be in the last decree dangerous, should war arise, to have India as a battlefield; and on grounds of military strategy, they are convinced that, sooner or later, we ought to occupy certain positions beyond our present frontier as outworks of the Empire. Therefore, advancing from Jacobabad, which is now our uttermost station on the Scinde border, they would proceed up the Bolan pass, through Shawl, into Afghanistan, and, leaving Kabul and Ghazni untouched, they would take possession of Kandahar and eventually also of Herat, and establish at these two points fortresses of exceeding strength, to be to India what the Quadrilateral had been to Venetia, strongholds such as no invader would dream of trying to mask. And the long process of a regular siege would, it is argued, be an almost hopeless undertaking in consequence of the natural poverty of the country, the distance of the enemy from their base, and the previous destruction of the crops of the besieged."

Events have amply proved which of the schools was correct. The picture painted by

Wyllie, in ridicule, might stand as a faithful record of what is being accomplished, indeed, is almost completed.

Mr. Wyllie's own opinion deserves reference, as a brilliant statement of the case from the "non-intervention" point of view.

"Were the Russian frontier," he said, "pushed forward from the line of Jaxartes to the foot of the Hindu Kush, were there war in Europe between England and Russia, or even if both these contingencies came upon us at the same time, there would still be many grave reasons for pausing before we fairly committed ourselves to the project of defending the British boundary by means of an advance into Afghanistan. In the first place, there is the nature of the country and its inhabitants, both so untractable that, except in the last resort, the task of dealing with them had far better be left to a rival or an enemy than undertaken by ourselves. It is a land, in Lord Wellesley's contemptuous phrase, of 'rocks, sand, deserts, ice, and snow,' and the men it breeds are warlike, turbulent, fanatical and perfidious. Take a small force into the country, and you are beaten; take a large one, and you are starved. Then there is the financial argument to be considered. The army that made its way up the Bolan pass in 1839, all counted, was only 19,000 strong, yet the Afghan war cost us from first to last fifteen millions sterling. Whence is to come the money for a repetition of the experiment? As it is, the finances of India are with difficulty kept at a bare equilibrium, and the ways and means for any extraordinary expenditure could only be provided either by an increase of taxation or an addition to the public debt. The latter alternative manifestly hampers the resources of the Empire for a future time of, perhaps, sorer need; and the dangers of popular discontent arising from the former are so great that, sooner than incur them, Lord Canning declared his readiness to dispense with the services of 10,000 English soldiers. Lastly, there can be no question that, however desirable from a strategic point of view the establishment of outworks at Kandahar and Herat might be, there are, *per contra*, certain solid advantages in the present concentration of our strength on the Indian side of the passes which would be forfeited, and some perilous responsibilities would have to be incurred, in connection with the proposed advance. For instance, the troops now quartered on our frontier are available equally for the repulse of foes from without and for the suppression of insurrection from within; whereas every red-coat dispatched beyond Jacobabad, and committed a hostage to fortune among an unfriendly race, would be so much strength taken from, so much anxiety added to, the internal garrison of India. That garrison would have to be largely increased. And whence are the men to be obtained?"

Sir John Lawrence was altogether against any steps which would inevitably arouse the suspicions and enmity of the Afghans, or violate the spirit, if not the letter, of our engagements with Afghanistan. In his opinion, whether

Britain advanced as friend or foe, the final result would be the same. Any advance, therefore, towards Kandahar or Kabul would be but the prelude to an occupation; Quetta and Kuram were mere stepping-stones to Herat and Kabul, in the event of a Russian forward movement. These positions, whose strategic importance he acknowledged, could not be garrisoned except at what would be a prohibitive expenditure of men and treasure, for the garrisons would have to be added to the existing army. Afghans in any considerable number would be dangerous, Goorkhas were not to be had, and Hindustanis and Sikhs would object to service in Afghanistan. To advance would be to dangerously increase the interval between our advance posts and our effective base, while decreasing the distance Russia would have to traverse. On the other hand, should the Russians elect to attack India, they would, on their way to the Indus, have to execute long and wearing marches through a most difficult and miserably poor country, inhabited by a bold and fanatical people, a country lending itself admirably to defence; would reach the field of battle—which could be selected by the British commanders—with their forces worn out and broken down. In a Russian occupation of Afghanistan, the former would run the risk of insurrection and of the tribes siding against her. Finally, troops massed along the frontier would be better able to control discontent than if locked up beyond the mountain ranges of Afghanistan.

"Taking every view, then, of this great question," to quote Sir John Lawrence's own words, "the progress of Russia in Central Asia, the effect it will, in course of time, have on India, the arrangements which we should have to make to meet it, I am firmly of opinion that our proper course is not to advance our troops beyond our present border, nor to send English officers into the different States of Central Asia, but to put our own house in order by giving the people of India the best government in our power, by conciliating, as far as practicable, all classes, and by consolidating our resources. I am greatly in favour of opening up lines of communication of every kind which, on full consideration, are likely to prove useful, so far as the means will permit; but I strongly deprecate additional taxation to any important extent, and I am greatly averse to increasing our debt on unproductive works."

Such were the views of the "non-intervention" school, which, though an advance has been made in search of a scientific frontier, prevail to this day.

The present-day opponents of any further British advance towards or beyond Kabul are influenced in their opinions by both financial and political considerations. Where is the money to come from to maintain such an army as would be necessary for an advance? And, should England defeat the Russians at some point on the advance, what would be the gain? The Russians would merely fall back into their own territory, while the English would have behind them the treacherous Afghans; and further, they say, chiefly British troops would have to be employed, since the Indians are averse to fighting in Afghanistan. The effect on India's exchequer would be ruinous; even now the smallest movements of troops, to quell unruly tribes, is costly, and causes disorganization of the internal transport.

Again, in Russia it is the *mujik* on whom falls the burden of taxation, while in India it is the agriculturist who suffers most. The imposing of further taxation, in either country, would be attended with danger. And even were the money forthcoming, the difficulty of waging war in the unproductive mountainous country or desert lands of Afghanistan would be equally great for either Power. No advance is to be advocated beyond Jalalabad, which offers a good position for the development of military defence, and also for the extension of railways. Should Russia then attempt to occupy Kabul, Britain could, from Jalalabad, supply arms and men to aid the Afghans in the defence of their capital. Indiscriminate creation of outposts is costly, and valuable troops are wasted in garrisoning them.

In answer to the theory that Russia, by pushing her way further into Afghanistan, will be able to obtain there innumerable recruits, who will aid in her further advance upon India, they say it is probable that the Afghans would prefer the better pay and the better treatment they would be likely to receive from the British. Finally, if Russia armed the natives, they would be as ready to plunder Russians as English, and in the end Russia would possibly find them more of a menace to herself than to her opponent.

The views of the "forward" school may now be briefly given. They maintain that Kandahar and Kabul should be occupied by the British, declaring that from these places a Russian invading army could be easily checked by a comparatively small force, who could destroy each detachment emerging from the narrow mountain passes. Those who hold the view that a further advance ought thus to be made, express the opinion that the cost would not be so great as anticipated. They say also it is not necessary to conquer and hold Northern Afghanistan. The Afghans could be readily enlisted as supporters of the British, if the latter offered to them a tribal, and therefore popular, form of government, in lieu of the oppressive rule of the Amir; such tribes as refused support could be easily subdued and disarmed.

Such, briefly stated, are the *pros* and *cons* of the question from the "advance" and "no-advance" point of view. Of late years a section of the British public has inclined to regard the Russian advance with equanimity, as in the interests of humanity and civilization, and so forth.

Afghanistan is in the unpleasant position of being "between the deil and the deep sea." She can no longer preserve a passive independence; for, as she has learnt from experience, she has no alternative but to throw in her lot with one or other of the two European nations between whose territories she is, unfortunately for herself, the sole remaining buffer. Whether Russia or England should be her ultimate choice as ally, the result to her own territory will probably be the same—namely, gradual absorption by the stronger Powers. Both these nations have, in fact, on various occasions given her cause for distrust. It is not so very long since England, in return for the support given her by Dost Muhamed during the Mutiny, declined to lend either men or money to his son, Shere Ali, when his succession was disputed; leaving him unaided to fight out his battles with his brothers, and only acknowledging him when, after a five years' struggle, he had eventually himself succeeded in establishing his supremacy. Russia, to whom later on he turned in desperation, proved herself no more reliable; for, although she promised him help and support, she left him to his fate when matters culminated in England declaring war against his country.

At present, of course, matters are on a friendly footing between Abdur Rahman and the Indian Government, but what may happen on the death of the present Amir is what no man can foretell.

There is no doubt that, when this event occurs, internal dissensions will ensue, and the final outcome, as regards Russia and Britain, is a matter beyond the power of prophecy. Possibly, however, even before Abdur Rahman quits this life, matters may have been brought to a climax by a Russian occupation of Herat, or of some other important point, and an advance towards the Persian Gulf; in which case Britain will be forced to a decision regarding the policy she intends to pursue for the ultimate defence of her Eastern Empire.

It must, however, be borne in mind that the Amir himself is not the chief factor in the problem which must at once receive consideration. Amirs may come and go, but the country and people remain. The general nature of the country from a physical point of view, its capabilities for offence and defence, and the characteristics of its inhabitants, especially of the warlike and still semi-barbarous tribes dwelling on its eastern borders: all these matters must necessarily have a bearing on future events. A brief survey of these points is therefore necessary.

The country consists almost entirely of

mountainous territory, and, with the exception of a projection on the north-east towards the Pamirs, is almost square in form. On this north-eastern frontier the great Hindu Kush mountains, extending for 400 miles in a south-westerly direction, rear a natural barrier between the Afghans and the Mongols, forming at the same time the water-shed of the Oxus, the Helmand, and the Indus. The passes in these mountains, all of them considerably more than 11,000 feet in altitude, are difficult, and in some cases almost impracticable; whilst the interior of Afghanistan itself, with its innumerable mountain fastnesses, is admirably suited for defence, and as a consequence is not easy of invasion.

Afghan Turkistan, the Herat province, with neighbouring Khorasan and Seistan, form the glacis of Afghanistan, just as Afghanistan is the outwork of India. Plains lead up to Herat on the Persian side. Abandon the Herat and Afghan Turkistan provinces to an enemy, and you enable her to sap up to the ravelin represented by the line Kabul-Kandahar, now acknowledged to be the British line of principal defence, which must be connected by rail, and again with the Indian railway system, to enable it to be held securely.

The question of supremacy at Herat has always been one of communications. A railway to Seistan should have been made years ago. Such a line would have rendered Herat secure against Russia, and Russia then would never have dreamt of a railway skirting Beluchistan to the Persian Gulf or Indian Ocean, such as she now intends.

It has been maintained, indeed, that in the mere matter of food an invasion of India would be impossible; that Afghanistan is able to produce scarcely enough for self-support, and that an army would there find no supplies. On the other hand, the most competent authorities now believe that with a proper development of roads and railways, and improved cultivation of the soil, the productive powers of the land would be materially increased. Colonel Mark S. Bell, who has a title to respect as perhaps the best military observer in these regions possessed by England, is of opinion that—within the time required to open up any part of Afghanistan they may occupy, and to prepare communications for a future advance—the Russians could support a considerable army in the Herat province. In ten years' time this district alone would, under good rule and State-aided irrigation, be capable of supporting an army of 60,000 men and more, and besides the Herat country, there are Afghan Turkistan and neighbouring Khorasan and Seistan. There would seem, therefore, to be no sound reason in the view largely held in bygone days, that the Herat valley was worthless.

"The Herat valley," wrote Sir George Ridgway,* "is by no means a smiling garden flowing with milk and honey. Surrounded by barren mountains, on the lower slopes of which are a few scattered hamlets, its central part, through which the river runs, contains the only valuable and culturable land. A strip on each side of the river, varying from two to five miles in width, is fairly well cultivated, and as the villages and fields here lie close together, and the principal roads run through them, the hurried traveller may be excused if he generalizes from what he sees, and imagines that the whole valley is equally cultivated. But if he were to follow one of the roads along the outskirts of the cultivation, he would be soon undeceived. As for fertility, if I remember rightly, the average yield of the cultivated land is only fivefold, or, in exceptionally fertile spots, tenfold. Trees are few and far between, for it is a rule, whenever Herat is threatened, to cut down every tree within a radius of five miles. The

* *Nineteenth Century*, October, 1889.

population is poor and struggling, while Herat city is a mass of mud hovels, sheltering some 5000 souls, exclusive of the garrison." *

It is said by those who deride the possibility of Russia being able to advance through Afghanistan, that they must depend solely on one line of communication—a single line railway, liable to interruption by the action of floods, snow, or moving sands; exposed to flank attack from Persia; liable to the raids of Afghan tribes, who would take arms against Russia. But Russia enjoys a great advantage in the fact that the population of Afghanistan is not homogeneous; the Hazaras, Turkomans, Aimaks, Heratis, and others are ready for the advent of Russia; the Trans-Caspian line will be provided with sidings, as on the Trans-Siberian Railway,

* "The exaggerated fears of Russian power and intrigue entertained by Ellis, McNeil, Burnes, and Wade, the flame of which was communicated by them to the British and Indian Governments, invested Herat with a fictitious importance wholly incommensurate with the strength of the place, and its position in regard to Kandahar and the Indus. To speak of the integrity of the place as of vital importance to British India was a hyperbole so insulting to common sense as scarcely to need refutation, and which ignorance of the countries west of the Indus, and inexperience of military operations in the East, could alone palliate" (Sir Henry Durand, at one time Military Member of the Viceroy's Council, and afterwards Lieutenant-Governor of the Punjaub).

to meet all possible emergencies; the difficulties of nature can be overcome here as elsewhere; Northern Persia is rapidly becoming Russian, and will at any rate probably act with Russia; the Afghan tribes will side with those who are strong. Beyond their railway terminus, the Russians would, it is true, have serious difficulties—those of transport through very difficult country; but these are not insurmountable.

There is some doubt as to the origin of the Afghan people. The first historical allusion to them describes them as a tribe dwelling on the western side of the Suliman range. At the present day the country is inhabited by the tribe known as true Afghans, otherwise the Abdalis or Durranis, by the affiliated tribe of the Ghilzais, not regarded as true Afghans, and by a number of other affiliated Afghan tribes, more or less independent and warlike, and collectively known as Pathans. The Ghilzais, who are probably of Turkish origin, although perhaps not numerically so strong as the other tribes, are without doubt the most powerful; and without their support no ruler could for long hold his own in Kabul. Their occupations are chiefly pastoral, but they make good fighters, and their commercial ability is by no means to be despised. As a whole, the Afghan people may be regarded as extremely patriotic, fanatical to a degree, somewhat avaricious, and not to be depended upon for fidelity to their allies. That it is possible to develop manufactures and other industries in their midst has been abundantly proved. Already at Kabul foundries and factories have been created on a considerable scale, where an unlimited command of men and money have enabled Sir Salter Pyne, a mechanical engineer employed by the Amir, to make great progress with the manufacture of arms and ammunition.*

The majority of the people profess Mohammedanism, and, as elsewhere noted, are exceedingly fanatical in their beliefs. The *mullahs* exercise great power. They have no priestly position—there is none in the Mohammedan religion—but are merely "learned in the law," their chief duties being to celebrate marriages and work out the intricate arithmetical problems presented

* Some time back the arsenal was capable of turning out 7000 Martini and 9000 Snider cartridges per day; a gun and rifle factory has been established; soap, candles, and boots are also manufactured; while gunpowder, shells, fuses, swords, as well as many other articles, can now be produced at the capital; and workshops have also been erected at Jalalabad.

by the Mohammedan law of inheritance. In case of war, especially a holy war, when Islam is considered to be attacked, the *mullahs* incite to disorder, zeal, and fanaticism, and then become all-powerful.

In addition to the country and the people, there is another, a still more important point to be considered, and that is the present relative positions of Russia and England in Afghanistan. It cannot be denied that the delimitation of a frontier which took place immediately after the Panjdeh incident was far from unfavourable to the Russians; and, with the Trans-Caspian railway completed to Kushk, Herat is practically within a week of the Caucasus and Moscow.* It has been said that Russia does not intend to "occupy Herat." Does anybody doubt that, with her railway extended to within seventy miles of that town, she is practically in possession

* "The Minister of War has made an experiment in regard to the movement of a detachment of troops from the Caucasus to the Trans-Caspian territory. The detachment was transported by railway from Tiflis to Baku, and by sea from Baku to Krasnovodsk, and thence by railway to Kushk, where it arrived on December 20 (January 1, N.S.). This experiment may be regarded as having been entirely successful, for it proves that in case of necessity a column forming the head of an army corps, sent from the Caucasus, might reach Kushka in eight days" (Telegram from St. Petersburg).

of the place? Her policy is to push on until the Hindu Kush range is reached, and to occupy the entire Herat province. This achieved, she would ere long be able, whenever opportunity offered, to attack India from her own territory. To quote the words of General Sobolev, Chief of the Asiatic Department at St. Petersburg: "It is in the logic of facts that the Hindu Kush, the natural boundary of India, should shortly form the frontier of Russia, and that the province of Herat should fall into Russia's hands."

The question of the moment is, Shall England look quietly on while this forward policy of Russia is carried out to its final issue, devoting her entire attention to the strengthening of her present defences in India? Or shall she herself make a further advance into the Amir's country, and prevent Russia's nearer approach to the Indian frontier? The principle so constantly affirmed by British statesmen, that Afghanistan is the "outwork of India," and "outside the sphere of Russian influence," will be hard to maintain, having regard to the steady progress which the Russians have been, and still are, making into the very heart of the country. The policy of preserving a neutral zone, so vigorously advocated by Lord Clarendon, is, in fact, every day becoming more and more impracticable. There is no doubt that Russia is bent on absorbing Afghanistan, and the question to which an answer is now urgently needed is, Shall Britain allow her to do so unchecked? To carry out the undertaking given to the Amir by Britain, *i.e.* to maintain the integrity of his country against aggression, is not only Britain's duty, but necessary for the safety of the Indian Empire, for the purpose of keeping Russia at bay; but it is a guarantee which the progress of events renders increasingly difficult of fulfilment. So far, Russia cannot directly threaten India, although she may squeeze Britain and force her into war. Should she, however, be permitted to advance as far as the Hindu Kush, affairs would at once assume a totally different aspect, and India would be directly threatened, and nothing but a most determined sortie from India, one involving the very greatest sacrifice in blood and treasure, could then possibly save that Empire.

With an advance into Afghanistan, in case of conflict with Russia, a large proportion of the Indian army would have to be moved from where they are now needed to maintain the peace of India, and the greater part of the military strength employed would be separated from India, not merely by the Afghan-Indian mountain defiles, but also by a large tract of Afghan territory, threatening seriously the long line of communications; and it has to be remembered that a modern army is such a complicated organism that any interruption in its communications tends to break up and destroy its very life. And should large bodies of men be needed at Quetta, Rawul Pindi, and various other frontier posts, there is no army *at present* available, without denuding India of its proper garrisons. Such an experiment in a recently conquered, impoverished, and overtaxed country like India would be a most dangerous one, especially at a time like the present, when, owing to the turn which events have taken in the South African campaign, Britain is in difficulties and her prestige low.

Britain has, of course, already made an important advance towards the Amir's country, in the search for a "scientific" frontier, which, however, recedes as she moves forward. After the Panjdeh incident, which created so much excitement in England, the construction of the railway from Sibi to Pishin was resumed, and the line opened in 1887; the Kwaja Amran range, the western limit of the Pishin district, was tunnelled, and a powerful post created in Afghan territory at New Chaman, the railway terminus. Here rails were stored ready to carry the railway forward to Kandahar. The construction of a great military road between the Indus and Pishin, *via* the Borai valley, was undertaken, while the fortified lines of Quetta were extended. Local opposition was met by military expeditions, troops being stationed in the new territories, to bring under British influence the country between the Amir's actual dominions and that of India. This occupation involved a large increase of the garrisons of Quetta and the Pishin valley. It may here be noted that there are already three railways connecting Quetta with Sibi—one up the Bolan pass direct to Quetta; another up the Hurnai valley to Bostan, in Pishin, twenty-one miles in advance of Quetta, and united to that place by a branch line; and a third *via* the Mushkaf valley.

By 1887–88 an increase of nearly 30,000 to the Indian army was found necessary, and in this quarter of the frontier as much as 43,000 square miles were added within fifteen years to the Indian Empire. In the north-east of Afghanistan fresh responsibilities were incurred on and beyond the Kashmir frontier; and the Kuram valley, abandoned in 1881, was reoccupied. In 1894 Waziristan was reduced to submission, roads were constructed, and fortified posts created. The occupation of Chitral followed, and made India and Afghanistan co-terminous. The next advance, if made, must be into Afghanistan itself.

Finally, before leaving the question of Afghanistan, it must be remembered that Russia has never entered into any undertaking to refrain from the invasion of Afghanistan; and that she considers herself free to treat that country not as a dependency of India, but as an independent State. Britain, moreover, has never formulated any declaration to the effect that an infraction of frontier would be a *casus belli.* That complications are likely to arise in the near future is a foregone conclusion. Even now, it is said, the Amir contemplates receiving agents at Kabul, and it will be difficult for Britain to prevent the advent of emissaries from both Russia and France. There may be less cause for anxiety so long as the present Amir holds the throne; but, as has been said, his death would probably be the signal for internal warfare, with what final results cannot be foreseen.

To turn now to Persia. Russia has her own plans with regard to that country. She desires an accredited agent at Kabul, but she is also ambitious of running a railway southwards, and obtaining a port on the Persian Gulf. The reason she advances, in pressing for such a port, is her alleged fear that Britain intends to extend her Indian line of railway through Beluchistan to the Persian Gulf, to join Germany in Asia Minor, and thus to complete the Indo-European system, and cut Russia off from the Indian Ocean. And so Russia advances her claim to a Persian port, "in order to be before the Germans." Her right to such a concession is becoming an article of faith, and on the banks of the Neva will shortly be considered as a sort of bureaucratic "Monro doctrine." There is no doubt that her occupation of such a port, by means of a railway, carried south and skirting Beluchistan, would be a most serious menace to India. The present Viceroy of India, Lord Curzon, some years ago regarded the concession of a port upon the

Persian Gulf to Russia by any Power, "as a deliberate insult to Great Britain; as a wanton rupture of the *status quo*, and as an intentional provocation to war; and he should impeach the British Minister, who was guilty of acquiescing in such a surrender, as a traitor to his country." This view can be well understood when it is considered that through Southern Persia, as has been frequently pointed out by those who have studied the subject, lies the easiest overland road from Europe to India. Afghanistan is a difficult country to cross, and, for many years to come, an invading army could only traverse the mountain passes of the Hindu Kush in comparatively small numbers. Beluchistan, on the other hand, with its vast expanse of level ground, desert though much of it be, offers much greater facilities, and Persia is the base for operations in this direction.

That Britain has some right to dispute interference in Persia will be readily seen when we glance briefly at the history of her connection with that country, and the interests involved.

The first intercourse between Britain and Persia was in the middle of the sixteenth century, when commercial relations were established with Teheran. Some time after this, an English traveller obtained permission from the Shah for Christian merchants to develop trade with the whole of Persia; and subsequently, when the expulsion of the Portuguese became necessary, a treaty was entered into between Persia and Britain, whereby to the latter was conceded the right to "keep two men-of-war constantly to defend the gulf." In the year 1800, when Russia and France were premeditating a combined attack on India, Napoleon, not slow to recognize the value of Persia in the carrying out of the scheme, sent envoys to Teheran to secure, if possible, the Shah's co-operation. Little result, however, was achieved, and subsequently England despatched officers to attempt an improvement in the Persian army, and to counteract the influence exercised by Napoleon's envoys; an alliance, offensive and defensive, being ultimately effected, whereby the Shah agreed to assist in the defence of India against the Western Powers. Notwithstanding this treaty, however, whole provinces were later on given up to Russia, to whom was granted the sole right to place warships on the Caspian. The Shah, indeed, invoked England's help, especially when he was compelled to yield Erivan and Nakhitchevan to his northern neighbour; but just as Shere Ali had been abandoned in Afghanistan, at the time of need, so now was the Persian monarch left to his own resources. No wonder that he came to the conclusion that "England's friendship and promises were of little avail in a pressing emergency."

Since the early part of the present century Russian influence has made itself increasingly felt. On two occasions Persia has, at Russian instigation, even attempted, though unsuccessfully, to obtain possession of Herat; and at the present time the whole of the province of Khorasan, in Northern Persia, may be said to be practically under Russian domination, a consummation in part effected by the completion of the Trans-Caspian railway. The population here, as in other parts of Persia, are discontented and ripe for revolt. The weak rule of the Shah, the corruption amongst officials, and the general bad government have engendered in them an antagonistic feeling towards their present rulers; a fact of which Russia, with her well-known faculty of ingratiating herself with Orientals, has not been slow to take advantage. The disadvantages to Britain in allowing a Russian absorption of Persia are obvious. India would be menaced at the weakest point of her frontier, British trade in Persia—and practically the whole of the carrying trade is under the British flag—would suffer extinction, and the present British line of sea communications, and the future overland route, would be threatened by the establishment of a Russian naval base, and the presence of Russian ships in the Persian Gulf. It is indispensable that Britain should retain control of the gulf, if she wishes to preserve the trade with Southern Persia, which she alone has been instrumental in developing, after having, at the cost of many lives, not to speak of immense sums of money, freed the coast from the depredations of the pirates and slave-dealers, who at one time infested the shores. The impossibility of England opposing Russia in the north with any degree of success, and the supreme importance to England of the command of the Persian Gulf, are now acknowledged. The Persian Gulf is, and should remain, a British lake. It has been so since the beginning of the century, and it is to be hoped that Britain will not recede from that position. That England to some extent realizes her responsibilities in this direction is evidenced by the fact that the gulf is patrolled by British vessels, so effectively, indeed, that the Persian and Arab coast population believe that England supports and maintains Persia's authority in the gulf.

The task of opposing Russia in Persia will be no easy one. At the present moment she is devoting to her interests in this country all the time and energy that she can spare from Far Eastern affairs. Immense sums are to be spent on the development of railway lines—primarily, if not entirely, strategic—which will bring the Russian armies within striking distance of the Perso-Afghan frontiers and of India by way of Beluchistan. It is probable that a railway will be carried, bit by bit, towards the Persian Gulf. If such a scheme be carried out, Herat may technically not be occupied, and the line may in fact avoid the town; thus Russia would diplomatically refrain from directly wounding the susceptibilities of the Amir and of Britain. But it is imperative that, *before* such a line can be constructed, Britain should safeguard her interests by developing her Indian railway communications, open Beluchistan and Seistan, complete her overland connection with Europe and, for further security, increase her land forces. Should these steps not be taken, and Russia be allowed to move in Afghanistan or Persia, as now is her intention, the consequence would require Britain to arm as a nation to preserve the Empire.

It is Russia's policy to take advantage of the slightest opportunity offered her by her adversaries, and she sees one now in the extremity of Britain. Has Britain forgotten how Merv was occupied while she was busily engaged in the Soudan? Is she prepared to sacrifice her Eastern Empire, so carefully built up, and giving such promise for the future, or is she ready to make the necessary sacrifices to defend that great Empire? If the present British apathy and ignorance of the situation in Asia continue, the great Eastern Empire which has risen like an enchanted palace, will as swiftly pass away. Nor would it avail for the whole nation to spring to arms; what is wanted is, not men, but a man—a leader.

CHAPTER VIII

RUSSIA IN CENTRAL ASIA

The present chapter will be devoted to a brief investigation of the causes which have led to the present domination of Russia in Central Asia, and to a slight outline of her progress, territorial and influential, in that part of the world; together with a consideration of her present limits and of probable future developments in her line of action, as those developments are likely to affect, directly or indirectly, Britain's Eastern Empire.

Russia's policy of expansion is of no recent growth. It has now been in progress for some centuries, and was in the first instance imposed upon her by forces of nature irresistible in their strength. To see what these forces really were, and to a certain extent still are, it is necessary to look into the natural characteristics of the country, the early history of the nation, and the condition of its inhabitants.

In the north, the land of the Slav consists of vast expanses of gloomy forest, alternating with icebound morasses and frozen lakes. These give place, in Central Russia, to the "black land;" vast plains on which corn is cultivated in large quantities; while in the south are the steppes, the more western of which are to a certain extent under cultivation, while those further east are nothing but dreary wastes, through which formerly roamed bands of nomads, plundering and murdering any hapless intruder who came in their path.

The whole country is practically destitute of roads, and locomotion and communication generally are therefore carried on chiefly by means of the rivers; sledges being employed during the long winter, whilst boats are used during the brief time of thaw, when for a few months the surrounding country is in a state of liquid mud. Russia's seas are of little practical use to her; for two of them, the Baltic and the White Seas, are icebound for six months of the year, whilst the Caspian is in reality merely a huge lake, and the Black Sea rendered of little value to the White Tsar owing to the fact that its approaches are commanded by foreign Powers. With regard to climate, the long and rigorous winter and the short, hot summer give rise to drought and famine, which, indeed, are probably never absent from the land.

With such a country and such a climate, it is little wonder that the people are apathetic and inert. Devoted to a superstitious idolatry, although nominally Christian, the average *mujik*, or Slav peasant, who may be taken as a type of the true Russian, averse to all labour, unwillingly gives his time to the tilling of the ground or to the care of the herds and flocks, indifferent to all higher considerations, and seeking solace in *vodka*. In Russia, to-day, the chief idea contained in the system of government is to obtain revenue from the masses, whilst at the same time keeping them as ignorant as possible. This policy differs radically from the British plan of rule in India, which at least attempts to establish a just and free system of government, and by education to fit the natives for the Imperial citizenship which officially was granted to them in 1858. The Slav peasants, known as Great Russians, compose the most important part of the population, both as regards numbers and the influence they exercise over the non-Slav races. From early times they have been of an inherently migratory nature, feeling no love for their homes, and always ready to seek fresh fields, if by so doing they could hope to better their lot, and escape, perhaps, from the monotony of their lives and their chronic state of poverty and serfdom. South and east they endeavoured to migrate, merely to fall into the hands of the marauding nomads. Then they pushed their way northwards, there to find only a frozen, barren country. Military settlements continually followed in the wake of the peasant migrations, and thus were formed the Cossack colonies on the Volga, the Don, and the Dnieper. Extension to the west was attempted, but here Sweden and Poland for a time barred the way, until, indeed, Peter the Great introduced Western ideas and methods, and organizing a peasant army, secured to his country immunity from the domination of those Powers. Towards the middle of the thirteenth century, the great movement of migration and expansion was checked by an incursion into Russian territory of Tartars, known as the "Golden Horde," from the northern districts of China, who, having carried devastation throughout Northern China itself, and thence through Turkistan and Bokhara, eventually made a descent upon Southern Russia, and subsequently carried their incursions to the very heart of the empire. For two hundred years they held dominion over the country, and, in order that the collection of taxes might be facilitated, did their best to put an end to the peasant migration and colonization. Even under the rule of Ivan III., who delivered Russia from the Tartar domination, the lot of the peasants was but little improved, and, with the despotism established by that monarch's grandson, Ivan the Terrible, in the middle of the sixteenth century, they lapsed into an even more abject state of slavery, their condition becoming worse and worse as time went on. Even under Peter the Great they were not much better off, and it is matter of history that, under the Empress Catherine II. (1762–96), absolute powers over the serfs were conferred upon the landlords, who were permitted to sell or give away any or all peasants over whom they held sway. The Empress herself, it is said, gave away many thousands to her own personal favourites. It was not till 1855, when Alexander II. came to the throne, that any serious attempt to improve their condition was made. That monarch, with intent to introduce some reform, set about the abolition of serfdom, to which end freedom was immediately granted to Crown serfs, whilst, as far as possible, those belonging to private landlords were allowed to recover their traditional acres on condition of paying dues to the late proprietor and taxes to the Crown. Theoretically the measure was entirely beneficent, but practically its effect has not been so satisfactory as was expected. The reform was, for one thing, too precipitately introduced, and the peasantry, after their long years of servitude, were not fitted to take advantage of it. Not only have they had to work equally hard, but they have been compelled to borrow money in order to pay the legal dues demanded, with the result that they are now as much serfs to their creditors as formerly they were to the landlords. Under these conditions their desire for migration, called "colonization" by the Russians, still lives; the wretched *mujik* has, in fact, no inducement to stay in his icebound, unproductive native country, and his readiness to leave it is evidenced by the eagerness with which he seized upon the opportunity offered him of migrating to Siberia, to which land of promise many thousands annually emigrate. The recent acquisition of Manchuria opens a veritable paradise for these downtrodden people, and there can be little doubt that, with the help of the new railway, immense numbers will in a short time make their way to this fertile and beautiful country, the "Garden of Russia."

The Russian Government, actuated by the same desire for expansion, for political purposes, have ever sought an enlargement of boundary. Ivan III. having to all intents and purposes overcome the Tartars, thus practically liberating his country from their yoke, it was left for his grandson, Ivan the Terrible, to carry on the war against them. He did not, however, rest on such laurels as this campaign brought him, but waged war also on Swedes and Poles. Later, that is to say, at the end of the seventeenth and the commencement of the eighteenth century, Peter the Great, aided by his *mujik* army, finally crushed Sweden and other enemies of his country, and proceeded to considerably enlarge his domain. His dictum was that Russia, at all hazards, must obtain access to the open sea; and finding her advantages in this direction limited to the Arctic Ocean, his great ambition was to open to her the Baltic and the Black Sea. Having effected his object so far as the Baltic was concerned, he then turned his attention to the Black Sea; but his expedition in this connection against the Turks not only ended in failure itself, but led to the loss of his previously acquired territories in a similar direction. It was not, indeed, till more than fifty years later, in the reign of Catherine II., that the Black Sea came under Russian control; and even now the benefit to her in this respect is greatly minimized owing to the command exercised over the straits by the Turks, supported by certain European Powers.

In 1800 the Russian Tsar, Paul I., carried away by Napoleon's brilliant successes, conceived the grand idea of co-operating with him in attempting the expulsion of the British from India; and the gravitation of Russia and Britain towards each other in their Central Asian spheres may be said to date from this time. The scheme, of course, was soon abandoned; but not without an attempt being made to carry it into effect. A body of Cossacks actually crossed the Volga, and the proposed invasion of India might have been seriously attempted had not difficulties of transport and commissariat checked the advance between the Caspian and the Indian frontier. These difficulties might possibly have been overcome in time; but the campaign was prematurely cut short by news of the assassination of the Tsar, and was never afterwards renewed. It was this scheme which first gave rise to the distrust of Russia which has never since ceased to influence the British nation, and which has caused the expenditure of millions of money, largely extracted from the natives, in the endeavour to secure the approaches, by way of Persia and Afghanistan, to the Anglo-Indian Empire.

By the time of Paul I.'s assassination, the Russian peasants, owing to the various Western campaigns in which they had taken part, had begun to recognize the fact that their condition at home was not what they had a right to demand, and, actuated by the example of the other and freer peoples with whom they had come in contact, they began to turn their attention towards revolutionary movements. The new Tsar, Alexander I., who had begun his reign with attempts at improvement amongst his subjects, later became fearful of revolution; and to prevent this, introduced repressive measures, which were still more stringently enforced in the time of his successor, Nicholas I. In this reign national risings took place in Poland and Hungary, but were put down with a ruthless hand. A war, for the purpose of championing Greece, was commenced with Turkey, and encouraged by success, the Tsar endeavoured to seize certain territories on the Danube. England and France, however, who had formerly been his allies, refused to countenance these aggressions, and took up arms against him, compelling his withdrawal. That he was unwise to provoke the hostility of his former allies he doubtless realized when the Crimean War took place.

A further campaign against Turkey was undertaken in 1876–78, ostensibly with the object of rescuing the Bulgarians and Roumelians from Turkish oppression. The real object, however, was to obtain possession of the two provinces, and to effect an occupation of Constantinople, which Russia has always coveted. The other Powers interfered, and Russia's scheme was frustrated for the time being.

Finding it impossible to further extend her empire in Europe, unless, as has been said, at the cost of many lives and vast expenditure, Russia turned her attention to Asia, in which continent she could foresee grand opportunities for empire-building. Yes! Asia was open to her! There, with the exception of England, she would find no Power prepared to oppose her schemes, no country with strength sufficient for its own defence. And Russia is gradually extending her empire in Asia. Siberia, previously acquired, she has developed and colonized, as we have seen; Manchuria has quietly passed into her hands; Caucasia is receiving Russian immigrants; Turkistan is in her possession; and Afghanistan and Persia are now about to enter upon a course of exploitation. Finally, she means to force her way to the sea, to a seaport on the Persian Gulf or Indian Ocean, where she can create another Vladivostock. With forethought, energy, and fertility of resource, Russia is leading the way, and showing the world how to conquer by railways. She alone has recognized how much more valuable are communications than mere army corps; how necessary in the conduct of a nation's affairs is a fixed plan. Russian railways, made by Russians for Russia, now run right across Asia, under Russian guard, from Moscow to the China Sea, and from Batum through Trans-Caspia to the Western gates of the Chinese Empire, and to the Herat *province* (not the town)—the key of Afghanistan, which is the outwork of India. Both in the region of the Far East and of Central Asia, the Russian railways are also gradually to be carried further south—through China to the Yangtze valley, and through Persia to the Indian Ocean. At the same time she is pushing her feeder lines southwards also into Europe's sphere of influence to gain a commanding influence in Turkey and Persia. New lines will join her present Trans-Caspian system with the Trans-Siberian railway, and with the European-Russian system, and thus provide alternative routes to the present inconvenient trans-shipment across the Caspian. Is there no danger to all Europe and to the United States in this constant extension of dominion and growing control of the world's highways?

Is it to be supposed that this continual absorption of Central Asian provinces is solely for purposes of commerce and colonization? Russia has already many thousand miles of country destitute of population, Siberia alone being spacious enough to meet her requirements in this respect for centuries to come. The inference is that, whatever may have been the moving power in the past, she is now influenced by political motives. And, indeed, she herself attempts no concealment as to her true aim. India to Russians is still the land of fabulous wealth. Her method of effecting her object, however, has undergone a change. The old idea of a direct military invasion of India has been, for the time at least, abandoned, and in its stead the plan has been adopted of commanding Central Asia, Persia, and Afghanistan, by means of railways, and of reaching India's north-eastern frontier by way of China. Probably only in the event of England showing a determination to offer opposition, at any sacrifice, would any immediate military demonstration be made towards the Indian frontier—"the vulnerable heel." The time is not yet ripe.

It is frequently pointed out that Skobeleff,

who talked of hurling "masses of Asiatic cavalry" into India, is said later to have recanted his earlier views, and to have ridiculed the idea of a Russian invasion of India, pointing out the insuperable difficulties of transport for the 150,000 men required, and asserting that the Russians would have to fight the Afghans *en route.* Skobeleff found it prudent to adopt this line. But Afghanistan, with orderly government, could in time raise considerable supplies, and the Afghans would side with the Russians, if they appeared the stronger. It may also be noted that the "masses of Asiatic cavalry," which have been so much ridiculed by certain British authorities, were not those already at the disposal of Russia, but those to be organized in Afghanistan and Persia and the borderlands generally. Therefore it is Russia's policy to develop the resources of Afghanistan, and as with this country, so with others in Central Asia. Where she can develop cultivation, she will provide storehouses for the time when she wishes to introduce an invading army. Where she can develop her railway systems, she will have the means of transport ready to her hand. She aims at re-creating the fertility of the

Central Asian steppes, and thus forming fresh bases for further advance. This difficulty of providing food for her armies has always been one of her hindrances, and she has hoped to find in some point abroad a territory where her troops could be fed, the necessity naturally growing as her advance proceeded. At first Tashkent was looked upon as a possible granary, then Bokhara, then Khojent, and the country between the Jaxartes and Oxus, known as the Garden of Central Asia. But now, at last, in the Herat province and Khorasan, granaries can be created of great value.

Any thought of a rising against her in Central Asia is out of the question. The Turkomans, Kirghiz, and other tribes, have been hopelessly crushed. They have nothing to hope from rebellion, no hope of support from England; whereas in India the case may one day be quite the other way. The British have some reason to fear an outbreak of close on three hundred millions of natives of India; the Russians none from the eight or ten millions in Central Asia. In the event of risings of individual tribes, Russia would no doubt find herself quite able to deal with them, as she did with the Akhal

Tekkés, and as she has done in innumerable other instances.

Her method of dealing with tribes, whom it is her object to subdue, presents a great contrast to that adopted by the British. The latter make a display of force, which has but little effect on the warlike natives, with the result that, so soon as the troops are withdrawn, disturbances again arise. Russia pursues quite a different plan. When she sends out a punitive expedition, no mercy is shown, even women and children being sacrificed in order to further her aim of a complete subjection. Consequently a single lesson of this nature amply suffices for the tribe concerned. The manner in which Caucasia and Central Asia have been subdued by the Cossacks is but an example of what, no doubt, Russia would be able to effect in any other portion of the territory she acquires in Asia.

Sooner or later, however, Russia must make her final blow. She may await the completion of her railways, the development of her territories, and a closer approach to British frontiers, before bringing matters to a climax; or, on the other hand, she may find favourable opportunity (such, for instance, as that provided by England's present pre-occupation in South Africa), may be forced by circumstances—"inexorable circumstances," the Russians term it—to hurry matters. Even as Constantinople was and is her aim in Europe, so in Asia is India the prize she covets. Peter the Great is reported to have said in his will (although the version containing the words is disputed), "Approach as near as possible to Constantinople and India. He who establishes himself in those two places will be the true sovereign of the world." And, whether the words are authentic or not, Russia has relentlessly pursued the scheme they indicate, using all means coming to hand in furtherance of it—extension of territory; subjugation of opposing tribes; treaties for favourable frontiers (*e.g.* after the Panjdeh incident); alliances; making and, when convenient, breaking of promises; construction of railway lines; acquisition of ports;—anything, in fact, likely to assist her. In the words of Sir Henry Rawlinson: "Any one who traces the movements of Russia towards India on the map of Asia, cannot fail to be struck with the resemblance which these movements bear to the operations of an army opening parallels against a beleaguered fortress."

And at the present moment the only remaining obstacle to be overcome is that supplied by the strip of mountainous territory in Afghanistan, or, if she elect to make her attack by way of Persia, the easily traversed plains of Beluchistan. A further occupation of Afghanistan, therefore, can only be looked upon either as a direct provocation of hostilities, or as providing her with a better position for future attack; for under no other hypothesis can such a move be explained. If commercial development merely were the object, there is plenty of room on the Asiatic continent for such development, without encroaching on India's defences. But even if purely commercial aims were in question, although Russia might be within her rights, Britain would be perfectly at liberty to combat her policy, so far as possible; for, although the latter early obtained a practical monopoly of the best markets of the world, she has thrown those markets open, welcoming all competitors, while Russia aims at exclusion, and replies to Free Trade by Protection, each step of her progress meaning loss to Britain. But commercial considerations are *not* at the root of the matter; and when Russia by further aggression or other unmistakable challenge has once thrown aside all further concealment of her designs, there remains but one course for Britain to pursue, and that is to attack her, not only in Asia, but all over the world, on sea or on land; and to do this while she is engaged in moving her troops over the space intervening between European Russia and India.

Russia has her own theories as to future possibilities. Doubtless her ideas on the subject have altered little since the time when Skobeleff, in his scheme of invasion in 1878 already referred to, said—

"Should our enterprise not result in complete success—that is, if a rebellion should not break out in India—and if we should fail to cross the frontier, we should nevertheless compel the British to keep the whole of their Indian army in Hindustan, and make it impossible for them to utilize any portion of it in Europe. They would, in fact, be compelled to transfer some of their troops from Europe to India. We could, in short, to a great extent, paralyze the land forces of England, either in a European war, or in the choice of a new line of operations from the Persian Gulf through Tabris to Tiflis in conjunction with the Turkish and Persian armies."

CHAPTER IX

THE DEFENCE OF INDIA

"For I hold it to be an essential principle that under no conceivable circumstance would it be compatible, either with the good faith of the contracting Powers or the safety of the Empire, that the agreement come to by us with Russia, on behalf of the Amir, in regard to the northern boundary of Afghanistan, should ever be modified or ignored. Any further approach of a great foreign military Power towards the confines of India would entail upon the latter country such an intolerable amount of expense in the shape of additional fortifications and other measures of defence as would become absolutely intolerable, and would be less preferable than any other alternative, however serious."—*The* MARQUIS OF DUFFERIN AND AVA, *ex-Viceroy of India, at the Guildhall, May 29th,* 1889.

"The more powerful Russia becomes in Central Asia, the weaker does England become in India, and, consequently, the more amenable in Europe."—A. SOBOLEV.

THESE words of Lord Dufferin and General Sobolev accurately place before us the present situation of Britain in India, whilst clearly

MAP ILLUSTRATING POSSIBLE LINES & BASES OF OPERATIONS BETWEEN CENTRAL ASIA & N.W. INDIA.

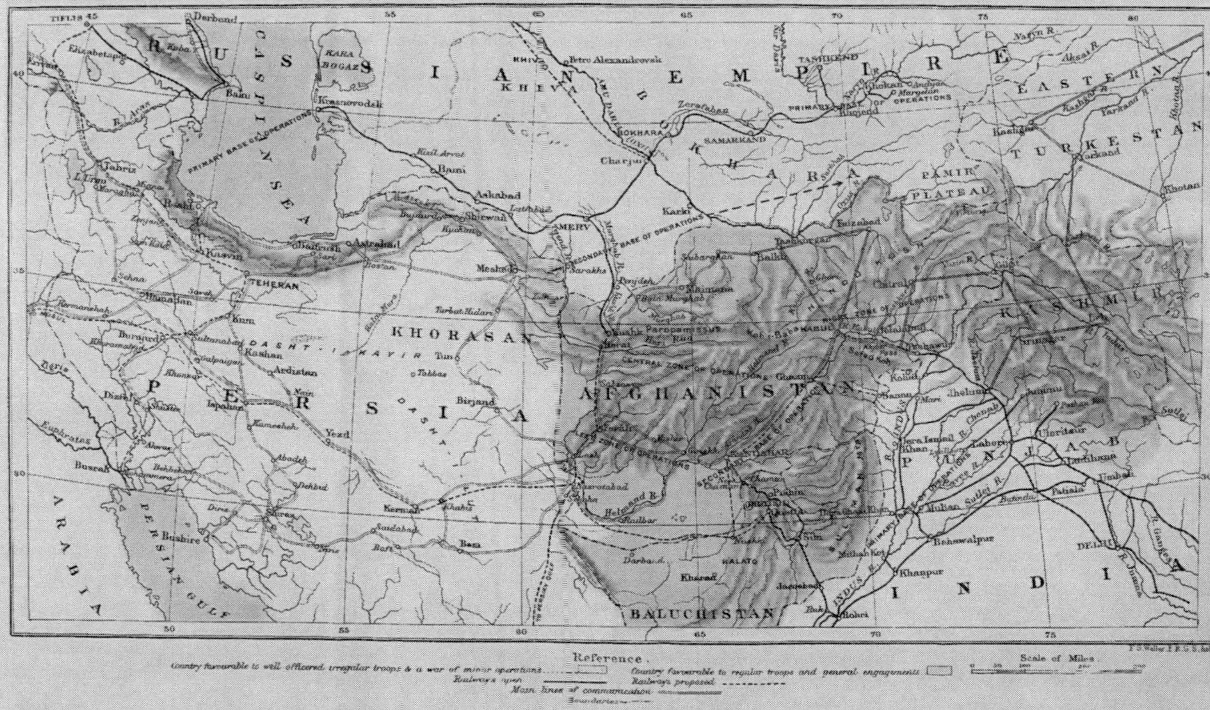

indicating her only possible course of action if the integrity of her Indian Empire (and with it the interests of her Eastern colonies) is to be maintained.

India may in fact be regarded as the centre or pivot of Britain's Empire in the East; and for this reason alone, setting aside all other considerations, must be defended against foreign aggression. It is not only British supremacy in that country itself which is at stake; the uninterrupted intercourse with her Eastern colonies, and consequently the well-being of the colonies themselves, would at once be threatened, should foreign invasion take place. Those who either ignore unpalatable truths, or advocate the policy of submitting to what they regard as the inevitable, and who adopt a line of conduct which must lead to Britain's gradual effacement in Asia, in preference to opposing Russia's onward march, are certainly not the men who have built up the British Empire, and they are not the men who will help to preserve it. There is no valid reason for Britain yielding her pride of place. It is true that her strength, as represented in her colonies, spread over the globe, is in great part beyond the immediate control of the mother-country;

while Russia, on the other hand, has complete command of her ever-increasing population and resources, and thus is able to concentrate her forces, whenever it pleases her, on the Indian frontiers. But Great Britain is no isolated Power. Her interests are the interests of countless thousands throughout the world; her wars —as evidenced in the case of South Africa—are not by and for herself alone; they are of Imperial importance, and she can depend on loyal support from all her colonies.

It is generally assumed in Britain and the United States that Russia, strong for defence—on account of its immense area, the homogeneous character of its people and their stolid patriotism—is peculiarly weak for purposes of offence. The vast distances, the incomplete communications, the barrenness of the country, the extremes of heat and cold, the inefficiency of commissariat and transport, the corruption and incompetence of the commanders and officers, are all adduced to prove the impossibility of an advance through Afghanistan or Beluchistan. But, as we have already said, the communications are being perfected, supplies can be grown, the Russian soldier can support any extreme of climate, and finally, life is cheap in Russia. "We have the men, you have the money," is the Russian cry. It may be taken for granted, of course, that if Russia were now from her present base to attempt a direct invasion of India across the whole extent of Afghanistan it would fail. But does any one in his senses suppose Russia is going to embark on such a foolhardy enterprise, when, with the experience of her continued success, she can, without sacrificing the life of a single Cossack, without any great expenditure, do now as she has done before, *creep on bit by bit*, so as to avoid arousing the susceptibilities of the British public? The Russians have made a close study of the British character, under the influence of a democratic Parliamentary Government. The apathy and indifference to everything except the safety of the present second, embodied in the sayings, "A long way off," and "It will last our time," are powerful allies of Russia, and well she knows it. She is more likely to embark on a war with Japan for Corea, or with Turkey, when opportunity offers, for the possession of Constantinople—a war which would find high favour in Russia as holy—and to gradually continue the absorption of Persia,

Afghanistan, Beluchistan, and China. She can gain what she wants by gentle sapping and mining, and the next steps are probably the perfection of her communications southward to the open sea, the Persian Gulf or Indian Ocean, leaving, perhaps, the *official* occupation of Herat and Afghan Turkistan till some later date. Such a step has always been considered in Britain as impossible, except on the hypothesis that it would at once involve Russia in war with England. Exactly such a situation has arisen. Are we prepared to meet it?

While the ability of Russia to disquieten India and to drain the finances on military expenditure has greatly increased, the British public has been fed more and more on Russian "assurances"—with what degree of success events in the Far East can tell—and has seemingly embarked on the attempt to create an African Empire, an Empire which is to stretch from the Cape to Cairo; an adventure which, as emphasized elsewhere,* means gradual effacement of Britain in Asia. Meanwhile, certain steps have been taken. The frontier defences of India have been made stronger, though not impregnable,

* "China in Transformation."

at Quetta and Rawalpindi; British railways run to New Chaman, within sixty miles of Kandahar, which is connected with Kurrachi and the whole course of the Indus. The masterful Amir, too, is friendly, and the wild, fanatical tribes are held down by an iron hand. But the Amir may die any day, and what then? Then will come still one more opportunity for Russia to further shake the British position in India, by acquiring a commanding position in Afghanistan and Beluchistan, and smoothing the way for the final stage—the preparation of the Indian populations for the advent of their northern "Liberator," the Mistress of Asia.

It is often said that the Russian troops in Central Asia are generally not equal to the British, or even the best Indian troops serving in India. The Central Asian officers are notoriously not the *fine fleur* of the service. The isolated life, the inhospitable character of the country, the feeling of exile, are too much for the ordinary Russian, a man of little culture and few resources. With the advent of the railway, however, the *morale* of the troops—the officers especially—will be raised. The corruption, the want of business ability and precision, the carelessness of Russian military officials, are always invoked by those who deride the possibility of any hostile movement on India. But, as has been said before, one thing the Russians possess, plenty of men imbued with an ardent, if somewhat loutish, patriotism, and officers in profusion, who have no qualms about sacrificing their men wholesale. Another advantage Russia has over Britain in the quarter of the world under discussion—throughout Central Asia, Persia, Afghanistan, as well as elsewhere in Asia—a superior and rising prestige. Compared with British methods,—the punitive expeditions, the bourgeois state maintained by her officials, the feeble diplomacy and futile talking of the Government,—Russia's methods of warfare,*—her showy Asiatic magnificence, her iron hand under the velvet glove,—impress the Asiatic, and her reputation in Central Asia is correspondingly great, probably in excess of her real strength. With the increase of the visible signs of power

* At the capture of Geok Tépé by Skobeleff there was an indiscriminate slaughter of 8000 Turkomans—men, women, and children. Such wholesale slaughter, which broke the spirit of the whole of Central Asia, is claimed by the Russians as not only cheaper, quicker, and more effective, but in the end more humane.

—her strategic railways and garrisons—must inevitably come a further rise in prestige.

The greater portion of the Russian army is quartered in her European possessions, especially in Russian Poland: in the Caucasus, she has a force of over 100,000 men on a peace footing; her strength in Central Asia and Siberia, till lately small, has been considerably increased, and with the aid of the railways can be augmented rapidly whenever wished. For service in the Amur province and Manchuria, troops are sent round by sea as well as overland by the Trans-Siberian railway. Until lately, before it was largely increased, the Central Asian force had work enough to do in Turkistan and Northern Persia, on the Trans-Caspian line, and in keeping open communications. How far it has been strengthened is not yet known, but there can be no doubt that large bodies of men are being moved to the Afghan frontier, the efficiency of the Trans-Caspian railway having recently been tested by an "experimental" despatch of a body of troops from the Caucasus to the frontier post of Kushk, near Herat.

As regards the railway, in case of any serious

move into Afghanistan, the single line will be improved by the provision of a large number of sidings, or by doubling the line. Khorasan, the northern province of Persia, would be annexed and strongly garrisoned — an easy matter. As has been already said, there is no chance of the Turkomans or other tribes rising, and this fond delusion, still cherished by some, had better be abandoned at once.

It is a favourite form of argument with English politicians to demonstrate the antecedent improbability of Russia embarking on an "invasion of India." They find consolation in the thought that millions would have to be spent on her Central Asian communications with Europe and Siberia, and that the lines would be financially unproductive. Granted; yet these millions are being spent, and why? Not for any wild adventure, such as a direct and brutal attack on India would be at present, but to strengthen her offensive power against that country through Afghanistan—the fulcrum of the lever which will open the way for her first to the Persian Gulf or Indian Ocean, and eventually to the Mediterranean. The whole aim of Russia's advance into Central Asia has been with this object, to be able to "squeeze" Britain in India through Afghanistan; and now she is in a fair way to taking yet another step in this direction—a further occupation of Afghan territory, and a move southwards by railway towards the Persian Gulf. The acquisition of Port Arthur has whetted her appetite for strategic positions on the open sea, and she now aspires to one on the Indian Ocean. Having succeeded in this policy in the past, is she likely now to desist, when at last she is in a position to exert a more powerful pressure than ever on India; when she will be still more strongly established as years go by? No, not unless Britain takes up the question of the defence of India in the only way in which it can be effectively done, by putting herself in a condition of complete counter-preparation; and this cannot be accomplished merely by adhering to the present expensive defences, and so awaiting "the inevitable" within our frontiers, but by adopting a bold and comprehensive policy. What that policy should be will be outlined later on.

The opinion is held by many that a passive defence within the Indian frontiers is all that is necessary to preserve the Empire, it being argued in support of this opinion that the cost is less, transport difficulties are practically nil, and that Britain, on her own territory, would have a great advantage over an enemy many hundreds of miles from their base of action. It may be conceded that the immediate expenditure would be less, but the eventual cost to Britain of such an inadequate defence would probably be very large—what, indeed, might not be its price! With regard to the third argument, Russia has already, by means of her railway lines, overcome many of the difficulties as to transport and communications. One of the greatest objections to the scheme of passive defence is that it presents so long a frontier line to the enemy on which to operate, whilst at the same time involving grave dangers in the event of a reverse. History has before now illustrated the fact that such a frontier line, even when elaborately defended, is by no means impregnable.

Another proposal is to depend on the Suleiman range as a barrier, carrying on a passive defence behind these mountains by means of entrenched positions at Pishin, Quetta, and other points. But, used merely passively, these advanced positions are of practically little value. If Russia were allowed to bring her troops as far as the neighbourhood of these posts, she could, whenever it suited her, compel evacuation, for she could outflank the garrisons, and thus cut off communication with the British base in India. Clearly then, Quetta, Pishin and neighbouring positions are only of value if used as a base for pushing forward active measures of offence.

Perhaps the greatest danger consequent on passive defence, either within the Indian frontiers or behind the Suleiman range, is that Russia is left free to push her way towards the Persian Gulf, and, as pointed out,* her domination in these regions is far from being desirable. It would mean the control and, later, the ownership by Russia of Beluchistan,—some day, as the Russians hope, of Afghanistan! In any case, to allow Russia to become the neighbour of India, whether through Afghanistan or Beluchistan, with only the Indus as dividing line, cannot but be considered a suicidal policy. Rivers, as is well known, do

* Chapter VII.

not constitute a sure defence. A further argument is that, should Britain decide to rely on the Indus as the line of defence, the garrison of India, vastly increased though it might be, could not conceivably be made equal to the task of opposing on such an extended line an army numbering perhaps 500,000 men;* and, when in Russian possession, the resources of Afghanistan in men and food supplies would enable such an army to be created and maintained.

In the writer's opinion, the true defence of the British Indian Empire is to preserve Afghanistan and Beluchistan as real barriers, which can only be done by developing and extending communications to Kabul, Kandahar, and Seistan. There is no alternative. The policy of passive resistance should be at once abandoned in favour of an active scheme, which would embrace the domination of Kabul, Ghazni, and Kandahar,

* "The greatest want, in my opinion—and, I know, in the opinion of the Commander-in-Chief—is an increase to the number of British officers in the Indian army. We have endeavoured to meet this by establishing a reserve of officers, but the attempt has been a failure. . . . Yet upon the outbreak of war we ought to increase the number of European officers with every unit of the Native army, and we should require some hundreds of officers for transport duties and various staff appointments in the field. Where to lay hands upon these officers is a problem that has not been solved" (Sir H. Brackenbury, late Military Member Viceroy's Council).

the establishment of outposts in the Hindu Kush, and the power to advance still further towards Seistan and Herat, should circumstances require. This view of the situation is supported by that of the strategist Hamley, who, so long ago as 1884, was of opinion that the defence of India would be best ensured by "a strong British Government at Kandahar, wielding an army whose advanced posts should be at Kabul and Herat, based on Karachi, with railway communication at least thence to Kandahar."

The Indus plains must be defended, but *actively* defended, in Afghanistan. It is no longer enough to merely block the mouths of the passes. The present mode of defence, effective where only untrained Afghans were concerned, would be of no avail against large numbers of trained troops, valuable as these passes are as natural barriers against invasion. A more active policy must be pursued too, if we are to take full advantage of these natural features of Afghanistan—the inaccessible mountains and difficult roads. Too much reliance must not be placed on irregular Afghan troops, who, disunited themselves, might at any time be persuaded by threats or promises to enlist under the Russian banner. The expenditure involved must be undertaken by Britain herself, for the force necessary to cope with the situation in case of war would mean the financial ruin of India. Indeed, that country is unable to defray the cost of the present inadequate defence of frontiers which is growing every year. We may have to create a Central Asian province, paid for mainly by British revenues. Finance ministers are at their wits' ends even now to meet the ever-increasing demands, and there is danger to India from financial disorganization, as well as from Russian policy. The question is one to tax the powers of the British nation. But the difficulty has to be faced.

The question of Afghanistan's internal power for defence against Russia is of vital importance as affecting the safety of India. The necessity for providing for the adequate defence of the Indus plains is apparent, and for this purpose it is necessary, having regard to the proximity of the Afghan hills (which might otherwise at any time be in the occupation of the enemy), to see beyond these hills, for without such sight one cannot act decisively but must grope blindly in the dark ; to hold the mouths of the passes ; to create defensive posts and positions (main valleys) within the hills, barring the passages through them; and, finally, to hold defensive positions in the plains to their rear, and so prevent all egress from them.

Afghanistan, as we have said, is a mountainous and therefore highly inaccessible country. Its advantages for defence, after the experience of South Africa, are obvious. Just as the mobile Boers, sheltered by their rocks and hills, with an intimate knowledge of the ground, are able to almost defy attack, so a body of even irregular troops, under British officers, would be able to hold the Afghan country for an indefinite period against an invader; whilst, if sufficiently trained, and especially if stiffened by regular troops, such as those of the Anglo-Indian army, the defending force could no doubt be rendered capable of even meeting the enemy in the open, if circumstances so required. At the present time the native Afghan troops are not only unreliable, for reasons already given, but suffer from the disadvantages of immobility and of being badly officered. Against trained European troops they would, as at present constituted, be practically helpless.

Taking into consideration the number of men which the provinces of Afghanistan could support, it may be concluded that the country as a whole could provide for an army of close on 200,000. A popular leader, with ample means at command, would probably find little difficulty in enlisting from amongst the different native tribes such a force of men, of fair, if not first-rate, fighting efficiency. Under efficient government, too, cultivation of the soil would increase rapidly. Even allowing for a much slower increase in agricultural production than has taken place of late years in the Indian frontier provinces, Afghanistan could probably, in five years' time, furnish sufficient food to provide for 250,000 foreign troops; and there is little doubt, having regard to the latest information, that, within ten years' occupation of certain districts and the completion of the necessary communications, an army of over 500,000, foreign and native, could be concentrated in the country. Is such an advantage to pass into the hands of Russia, while England looks on and submits to "the inevitable"? If Britain continues to maintain her position of passive defence, refusing to safeguard her Empire by herself pushing forward a barrier against aggression, she will eventually find that further passive defence, or indeed any defence at all, is impossible.

To allow the fighting strength of Afghanistan to fall into the hands of Russia would be a two-fold mistake, for it would not only deprive Britain of valuable allies, but would add just so much strength to Russian power for mischief. It is said that the Afghans would be opposed to a British advance. Much, however, can be accomplished by a skilful diplomacy Probably a few easily suppressed risings would be the only result, whilst the majority would soon become contented and happy under a beneficent rule. Had Afghanistan been under British rule since 1842, it would long ere this have been in as orderly a condition as are Britain's Indian provinces; and, indeed, there is reason to believe that an improved system of taxation, which would be possible under a settled government, would in a single generation completely alter the condition of the country and people. Should Russia, on the other hand, obtain the ascendency, she would then find the absorption of Persia and Beluchistan an easy matter, and the further strengthening of her maritime bases and navy in Asia would then confer on her almost limitless power in the East.

One of the most natural directions for Russia's advance is undoubtedly that from Balkh to Kabul, this being the most direct road to the capital. In conjunction with this route, however, there is another and more practicable line, passing through productive country, and presenting few physical obstacles—that from Herat by way of Farah to Kandahar, and this is certain to be the route taken by the Russians. The mountainous northern zone is not so improbable a line of attack on India as has commonly been supposed, being accessible on the enemy's side at several points. On the British side a railway line connects Peshawar, the northern terminus, with Karachi, as well as with Calcutta. It is necessary not only to defend the passes here, but to develop communications beyond, an end best achieved by means of a railway to Kabul. The central zone—Ghazni, Bannu, Dera Ismail Khan—is another possible route for an attacking force, and it has to be borne in mind that surprises by means of hill roads are easy of accomplishment.

The question is, how far shall Russia be allowed to advance before England not merely raises her voice in protest, but places an insurmountable obstacle in her path? The Hindu Kush and the chief provinces, at least, should not be allowed to fall into the Tsar's hands. To give up any one of the provinces of Afghanistan to Russia is to weaken the defence of the entire country, and this applies especially to Herat, Kabul, or Kandahar. Any one of these places yielded to the enemy, provides that enemy with an opportunity for further strengthening themselves; while, on the other hand, if occupied first by the defenders, those defenders will hold an inestimable advantage.

The province of Herat offers incalculable facilities to an invader having designs on India. The province, as we have already said, as the key to Afghanistan has been called, not inaccurately, "the key to India." The appellation is easy to understand. To recapitulate its advantages: it is fertile, and capable of supporting a large army; it dominates the roads leading to Kabul, Kandahar, Ghazni, and other important towns, thus indirectly commanding the passes to India; and its natural features make it at once a barrier or a menace, according to the possessor. Rawlinson considered it of such importance that he expressed his willingness to give up all Afghanistan rather than allow Herat to be controlled by the Russians. In his pithy phrase, Herat and Kandahar were the Malakoff and Mamelon of India. The pivot of the whole Eastern question, in Rawlinson's view, was that Britain cannot afford to expose Herat to the risk of being taken by a Russian *coup de main.* "Russia in possession of Herat," he said, "would have a grip on the throat of India."

The main length of frontier to be defended between Faizabad and Herat, and that from Peshawar to Peshin are about the same—600 miles. There is a vital difference, however, in the two cases. In the former the real fighting front extends from the neighbourhood of Kabul to that of Kandahar, a distance of not more than 350 miles, the greater part covered by hills, whose main passes alone it is necessary to hold; in the latter, the whole extent of 600 miles of frontier line must be held, because of its comparative vulnerability.

The essential difference between the defence of the two lines is at once apparent. In the one case, conducted from the proper side of the passes, the configuration of the deep intricate hills allows the difficult roads penetrating them, closed by snow for three months in the year, to be economically defended by field armies well-placed in secure positions so as to block the outlets; their mouths under observation, the passes themselves can be blocked and held at favourable points. In the other it is conducted from the wrong side of the passes. Here the fronting barrier of hills is passable at many points, which can be blocked only by a most costly expenditure of force; and facing the narrow ragged screen of hills there are elevated plateaux and valleys favourable to the movements and concentration of troops, after due preparation of roads and depôts.*

Preparation for possible war should no longer be neglected by Britain. Fortified posts should be established in the Afghan territory, and depôts and magazines placed in such positions as are dictated by the geographical conditions of the country, having regard especially to the question of cultivation of the soil, a consideration affecting the future support of an army. Suitable

* Colonel Mark S. Bell, *R.U.S. Journal*, 1885.

positions for such depôts are to be found at the great centres of commercial activity—Kabul, Ghazni, Kandahar, Farah, Balkh, Herat, and other places.* It is essential that these points, necessary to the organization of field armies, their administration, and maintenance, be held by troops, though not necessarily by fortifications. An offensive-defensive plan of campaign, above all, requires for its efficient prosecution railways: from Peshawar to Kabul; from the Indus-Bolan line, *viâ* Nushki and south of the Helmand, through Baluch territory to Seistan, with lines to Kandahar, Farah, and Kabul; a direct military line from Chaman to Kandahar; and, eventually, a southern extension from Seistan to the Persian Gulf. Seistan, the watch-tower of Beluchistan and Khorasan, at the bend of the Helmand, is the one large oasis between Khorasan and the Gulf, the others to the south being of less importance.

The cost of construction of such lines would inevitably be heavy, but the expenditure is necessary, for it would secure the protection and increased prosperity of the Indian Empire. The

* On the map the bases of possible operations are shown, and the main lines of communications by double lines.

value of commercial-strategic railways does not seem to be understood in England as elsewhere—for instance, in Germany and Russia; and Britain will perhaps too late find out her mistake if, from motives of economy, she continues to favour merely commercial lines. The Trans-Siberian railway is an instance of the value of a line not only commercial but strategic in its objects. Railways, rather than mere armies, will decide the fate of India, and ultimately of Asia. The Russians never ask, "Will it pay?" They know it will *eventually* pay them. When Russia is extending her lines from the Caspian to Afghanistan and the Persian Gulf, and through China to the Yangtze valley, Britain cannot afford to sit still looking always for immediate results. She should reply by a direct overland line from Quetta to Seistan, and thence, *viâ* Kerman, to Ispahan, Mosul and onward, with branches. In time of war these railways would be absolutely necessary for the transport of such an organization as a modern army, and the incalculable importance of constructing such lines while there is yet time should cause all objections to be put aside.

Not only Britain, but Europe and the United

States, have a vital interest in barring further Russian progress in Central Asia. The danger of Russian ascendency, and consequently of the decline of British power in the East, is not yet realized. As was foreseen many years ago, the growth of Russia in the East threatens, though indirectly, the whole of Europe; for once firmly established in Asia Minor, Constantinople would be in imminent danger, the 'commerce of the Mediterranean would eventually fall into her hands, and she would command, not merely the Indo-European overland highway, but the canal through the Isthmus of Suez. All the more dangerous, too, as Russian ascendency in China is daily increasing, and at an alarming pace.

Hitherto it has been left to Britain alone to oppose Russia in the East, in doing which she has also been serving the interests of others. It would be wise for the European nations and the United States, whose interests are involved, not to oppose, but to join Britain in safeguarding those interests, and especially in defending that great overland highway of the nations between East and West, the maintenance of which, as an open trade route, is of such vast importance to European and American trade.

In order to defend her Asiatic interests, Europe can no longer depend exclusively on the Suez Canal line of communication. She needs also a more fully developed overland route—a railway line through Mesopotamia; and this not only for political but for commercial purposes. Such a railway would pass through fertile country, possessing a favourable climate, and populated in great part by agriculturists. By developing this region, Europe would be merely advancing her commercial interests, and for this purpose, almost as much as for political reasons, it is necessary to combat Russian policy. Between the Mediterranean and the Indian frontier lawlessness and oppression at present prevail, and the introduction of a more civilized control is a necessity of the age, and would be welcomed by the world at large. The cost of constructing such a line, roughly estimated, would be about forty millions sterling.

Not merely Russia and Britain but Germany also is now involved in Asia, by reason of her economic interests and railway enterprises in Asiatic Turkey and the Far East. Germany, the neighbour of Russia in Europe,—Germany, always ready for a deal. Shortly Britain in

India will be bordered on the east by Russia and France, and on the west by Russia and Germany. Under such circumstances, she can no longer avoid the burdens imposed on great land-powers, and must become a strong military State, especially as Russia, Germany, and France are now enormously increasing their naval strength.

The legitimate expansion of Russia does not now lie southwards. As trade outlets she has the Black Sea in Europe and the China Sea and Pacific in the Far East. It is not, cannot be, for any commercial purpose that she seeks to reach the Persian Gulf or Indian Ocean, but to create a powerful naval base and arsenal halfway to the Far East, with a great Hinterland behind, opened by Russian railways, as she has done at Port Arthur.

Forty years ago the Austrian War Minister predicted that Russia would try to reach the open sea by operating through Asia, as she has done.

"She will not reach the shores of the Persian Gulf in one stride," said this far-seeing statesman, "or by means of one great war; but, taking advantage of continental complications, when the attention and energy of European States are engaged in contest more nearly concerning them, she will endeavour to reach the Persian Gulf step by step—by annexing separate districts of Armenia, by operating against Khiva and Bokhara, and by seizing Persian provinces. . . . The growth of Russia in the East," he continued, "threatens, though indirectly, the whole of Europe, as well as the States named above; for if she were firmly established in Asia Minor, the real apple of discord, Constantinople, would be in imminent danger, all the commerce of the Mediterranean would fall into her hands, and she would command the canal through the Isthmus of Suez. . . . Whatever the commercial value of the canal to Central Europe, there is no doubt that it is secondary in importance to the Euphrates valley, which affords the only means of stemming Russian advances in Central Asia, and which directly covers the Suez Canal."

Certainly events in Central Asia and the Far East serve to show the wisdom of the conclusion arrived at so many years ago by this eminent statesman. The expansion of the Northern Colossus—more Oriental than European, whose heart of Empire lies in Central Asia—into China and towards the natural zone of influence of Europe; her determination to control commerce, religion, and communications, are grave dangers for all other nations, and more especially the Anglo-Saxon peoples. Unchecked, they would lead to the subjugation of Europe by Asia. The danger is clear to any one who will take up the map. Russia already becoming a paramount power in Northern China; Russia with a port on the Persian Gulf or Indian Ocean treated as a right beyond question; Russia connecting Central Asia with the Persian Gulf by railways, from Askabad southwards, and from Tiflis by Kars and the Turko-Persian frontier, thus making herself independent of the Dardanelles and the Suez Canal, and cutting into the direct Indo-European line of overland communication. A conflict between East and West for the dominion of the old world is imminent. Slav and Saxon must contend for supremacy, even for equality, and upon the skill and determination of the two opponents hangs the future of Asia, and not only of Asia but of Europe.

APPENDIX

In 1864 the Russian Chancellor, Prince Gortschakoff, issued his famous circular note, directed against the suspicions entertained in Britain regarding the Russian advance in Central Asia, and justifying the Russian forward movement.

(Circulaire.)

"St. Petersbourg, le 21 Novembre, 1864.

"Les journaux Russes ont rendu compte des dernières opérations militaires exécutées par un détachement de nos troupes dans les régions de l'Asie Centrale avec un succès remarquable et des résultats importants.

"Il était à prevoir que ces évènements exciteraient d'autant plus l'attention du public étranger qu'ils se passent dans des contrées à peine connues.

"Notre auguste Maître m'a ordonné de vous exposer succinctement, mais avec clarté et précision, la position qui nous est faite dans l'Asie Centrale, les intérêts qui servent de mobile à notre action dans ces contrées, et le but final que nous y poursuivons.

"La position de la Russie dans l'Asie Centrale est celle de tous les Etats civilisés qui se trouvent en contact avec des peuplades à demi-sauvages, errantes, sans organisation sociale fixe.

"Il arrive toujours en pareil cas que l'intérêt de la sécurité des frontières et celui des relations de commerce exigent que l'Etat plus civilisé exerce un certain ascendant sur des voisins que leurs mœurs nomades et turbulentes rendent fort incommodes.

"On a d'abord des incursions et des pillages à réprimer. Pour y mettre un terme on est forcé de réduire à une soumission plus ou moins directe les peuplades limitrophes.

"Une fois ce résultat atteint celles-ci prennent des habitudes plus tranquilles, mais elles se trouvent à leur tour exposées aux aggressions des tribus plus éloignées.

"L'Etat est obligé de les defendre contre ces déprédations et de châtier ceux qui les commettent. De là la nécessité d'éxpéditions lointaines, coûteuses, périodiques, contre un ennemi que son organisation sociale rend insaisissable. Si l'on se borne à châtier les pillards et qu'on se retire, la leçon s'efface bientôt ; la retraite est mise sur le compte de la faiblesse ; les peuples Asiatiques en particulier ne respectent que la force visible et palpable ; la force morale de la raison et des intérêts de la civilisation n'a point encore de prise sur eux. La tâche est donc toujours à recommencer.

"Pour couper à ces désordres permanents ou établir quelques points fortifiés parmi les populations ennemies, on exerce sur elles un ascendant qui peu à peu les réduits à une soumission plus ou moins forcée.

"Mais au delà de cette seconde ligne d'autres peuplades plus éloignées encore viennent bientôt provoquer les mêmes dangers et les mêmes répressions.

"L'Etat se trouve donc dans l'alternative ou d'abandonner

ce travail incessant et de livrer ses frontières à des désordres perpétuels qui y rendent toute prospérité, toute sécurité, toute civilisation impossible, ou bien d'avancer de plus en plus dans la profondeur de contrées sauvages où à chaque pas qu'il accomplit les distances accroissent les difficultés et les charges auxquelles il s'expose.

"Tel a été le sort de tous les pays qui ont été placés dans les mêmes conditions. Les Etats-Unis en Amérique, la France en Algérie, la Hollande dans ses Colonies, l'Angleterre aux Indes; tous ont été inévitablement entraînés à suivre cette marche progressive où l'ambition a moins de part que l'impérieuse nécessité et où la plus grande difficulté consiste à savoir s'arrêter.

"C'est aussi la raison qui a conduit le Gouvernement Impérial à s'établir d'abord d'un côté sur la Syr-Daria, de l'autre sur le Lac Issik-Kul, et à consolider ces deux lignes par des forts avancés qui peu à peu ont pénétré au cœur de ces régions lointaines sans cependant parvenir à établir au delà la tranquillité indispensable à la sécurité de nos frontières.

"La cause de cette instabilité réside d'abord dans le fait qu'entre les points extrêmes de cette double ligne il y a un immense espace inoccupé, où les invasions des tribus pillardes continuent à paralyser toute colonisation et toute commerce par caravanes; ensuite dans les fluctuations perpétuelles de la situation politique de ces contrées, où le Turkestan et le Khokand tantôt réunis, tantôt séparés, toujours en guerre, soit entre eux, soit avec le Bokhara, n'offraient aucune possibilité de relations fixes ni de transactions régulières quelconques.

"Le Gouvernement Impérial s'est donc vu placé, malgré

lui, dans l'alternative que nous avons indiquée, c'est-à-dire, ou de laisser se perpétuer un état de désordre permanent qui paralyse toute sécurité et tout progrès, ou de se condamner à des expéditions coûteuses et lointaines sans aucun résultat pratique et qu'il faut toujours recommencer, ou enfin d'entrer dans la voie indéfinie de conquêtes et d'annexions qui a conduit l'Angleterre à l'Empire des Indes, en cherchant à soumettre l'un après l'autre, par la force des armes, les petits Etats indépendants dont les mœurs pillardes et turbulentes et les perpétuelles révoltes ne laissent à leurs voisins ni trêve ni repos.

"Ni l'un ni l'autre de ces alternatives ne répondait au but que s'est tracé la politique de notre auguste Maître, et qui est non d'étrendre hors de toute proportion raisonnable les contrées soumises à son sceptre, mais d'y asseoir sa domination sur des bases solides, d'en garantir la sécurité et d'y développer l'organisation sociale, le commerce, le bien-être et la civilisation.

"Notre tâche était donc de rechercher un système propre à atteindre ce triple but.

"A cet effet les principes suivants ont été posés :—

"1. Il a été jugé indispensable que les deux lignes fortifiées de nos frontières, l'une partant de la Chine jusqu'au Lac Issik-Kul, l'autre partant de la Mer d'Aral le long de la Syr-Daria, fussent réunies par des points fortifiées de manière à ce que tous nos postes fussent à même de se soutenir mutuellement et ne laissassent aucun intervalle par où pussent s'effectuer impunément les invasions et les déprédations des tribus nomades.

"2. Il était essentiel que la ligne ainsi complétée de nos forts avancés fût située dans une contrée assez fertile, non seulement pour assurer leur approvisionnement, mais aussi pour faciliter la colonisation régulière qui seule peut préparer au pays occupé un avenir de stabilité et de prospérité, en gagnant à la vie civilisée les peuplades avoisinantes.

"Enfin, 3. Il était urgent de fixer cette ligne d'une manière définitive afin d'échapper aux entraînements dangereux et presque inévitables qui de répression en représailles pouvait aboutir à une extension illimitée.

"Dans ce but il fallait poser les bases d'un système fondé non seulement sur la raison qui peut être élastique, mais sur les conditions géographiques et politiques qui sont fixes et permanentes.

"Ce systeme nous était indiqué par un fait très simple, resultant d'une longue expérience, c'est-à-dire, que les tribus nomades, qu'on ne peut saisir ni châtier, ni contenir efficacement, sont pour nous le voisinage le plus incommode, et que par contre les populations agricoles et commerçantes, fixées au sol et dotées d'un organisme sociale plus développé, nous offrent la chance d'un voisinage tolérable et de relations perfectibles.

"La ligne de nos frontières devait donc englober les premières, elle devait s'arrêter à la limite des secondes.

"Ces trois principes donnent l'explication claire, naturelle et logique des dernières opérations militaires accomplies dans l'Asie Centrale.

"En effet, la ligne primitive de nos frontières le long de la Syr-Daria jusqu'au Fort Perovski d'un côté, et de l'autre jusqu'au Lac Issik-Kul, avait l'inconvénient d'être presque à la limite du désert. Elle était interrompue sur un immense espace entre les deux points extrêmes, elles n'offrait pas assez de ressources à nos troupes et laissait en dehors des tribus sans cohésion avec lesquelles nulle stabilité n'était possible.

"Malgré notre repugnance à donner à nos frontières une plus grande étendue, ces motifs avaient néanmoins été assez puissants pour déterminer le Gouvernement Impérial à établir cette ligne entre le Lac Issik-Kul et la Syr-Daria, en fortifiant la ville de Chemkent récemment occupée par nous.

"En adoptant cette ligne nous obtenons un double résultat. D'un côté la contrée qu'elle embrasse est fertile, boisée, arrosée par de nombreux cours d'eau ; elle est habitée en partie par des tribus Kirghiz qui ont déjà reconnu notre domination ; elle offre donc des éléments favorables à la colonisation et à l'approvisionnement de nos garnisons. De l'autre elle nous donne pour voisins immédiats les populations agricoles et commerçantes du Khokand.

"Nous nous trouvons en face d'un milieu social plus solide, plus compact, moins mobile, mieux organisé ; et cette considération marque avec une precision géographique la limite où l'intérêt et la raison nous prescrivent d'arriver et nous commandent de nous arrêter, parce que d'une part toute extension ultérieure de notre domination rencontrant désormais non plus des milieux inconstants, comme les tribus nomades, mais des Etats plus régulièrement constitués, exigerait des efforts considérables et nous entraînerait d'annexion en annexion dans des complications incalculables—et que d'autre part ayant désormais pour voisins de pareils Etats malgré leur civilisation arriérée et l'instabilité de leur condition politique, nous pouvons néanmoins esperer que des relations régulières pourront un jour se substituer pour l'avantage commun aux désordres permanents qui ont paralysé jusqu'ici l'essor de ces contrées.

“Tels sont, Monsieur, les intérêts qui servent de mobile à la politique de notre august Maître dans l’Asie Centrale ; tel est le but final que les ordres se Sa Majesté Impériale ont tracé à l’action de son Cabinet.

“Vous êtes invité à puiser dans ces considérations le sens des explications que vous fournirez au Gouvernement auprès duquel vous êtes accredité, si vous étes interpellé ou si vous voyez s’accréditer des suppositions erronées quant à notre action dans ces contrées lointaines.

“Je n’ai pas besoin d’insister sur l’intérêt évident que la Russie à ne pas agrandir son territoire et surtout à ne pas se créer aux extrémités des complications qui ne peuvent que retarder et paralyse son développement intérieur.

“Le programme que je viens de tracer rentre dans cet ordre didées.

“Bien souvent durant ces dernières années on s’est plu à assigner pour mission à la Russie de civiliser les contrées qui l’avoisinent sur le continent Asiatique.

“Les progrès de la civilisation n’ont pas d’agent plus efficace que les relations commerciales. Celles-ci pour se développer exigent partout l’ordre et la stabilité, mais en Asie elles réclament une transformation profonde dans les mœurs. Il faut avant tout faire comprendre aux peuples Asiatiques qu’il y a plus d’avantage pour eux à favoriser et assurer le commerce des caravanes qu’à les piller.

“Ces notions élémentaires ne peuvent pénétrer dans la conscience publique que là où il y a un public, c’est-à-dire un organisme social et un Gouvernement qui le dirige et le représente.

“Nous accomplissons la première partie de cette tâche en portant notre frontière à la limite où se rencontrent ces conditions indispensables.

"Nous accomplissons la seconde en nous attachant désormais à prouver aux Etats voisins par un système de fermeté quant à la répression de leurs méfaits, mais en même temps de modération et de justice dans l'emploi de la force et de respect pour leur indépendance, que la Russie n'est pas leur ennemi, qu'elle ne nourrit à leur égard aucune vue de conquête, et que des relations pacifiques et commerciales avec elle sont plus profitables que le désordre, le pillage, les représailles et la guerre en permanence.

"En se consacrant à cette tâche, le Cabinet Impérial s'inspire des intérêts de la Russie. Il croit servir en même temps les intérêts de la civilisation et de l'humanité. Il a droit de compter sur une appréciation équitable et loyale de a marche qu'il poursuit et des principes qui le guident.

"(Signé) "GORTSCHAKOFF."

THE WILL OF PETER THE GREAT,

As given in "Des Progrès de la Puissance Russe," by M. Lesur; published in Paris in 1812.

I. Neglect nothing which can introduce European manners and customs into Russia, and with this object gain the co-operation of the various Courts, and especially the learned men of Europe, by means of interesting speculations, by philanthropic and philosophical principles, or by any other suitable means.

II. Maintain the State in a condition of perpetual war, in order that the troops may be inured to warfare, and so that the whole nation may always be kept in training and ready to march at the first signal.

III. Extend our dominions by every means on the north along the Baltic, as well as towards the south along the shores of the Black Sea; and for this purpose:—

IV. Excite the jealousy of England, Denmark, and Brandenburg against the Swedes, by means of which these Powers will disregard any encroachments we may make on that State, and which we will end by subjugating.

V. Interest the House of Austria in the expulsion of the Turk from Europe, and under this pretext maintain a permanent army and establish dockyards on the shores of the Black Sea, and thus, by ever moving forward, we will eventually reach Constantinople.

VI. Keep up a state of anarchy in Poland, influence the national assemblies, and above all regulate the election of its kings; split it up on every occasion that presents itself, and finally subjugate it.

VII. Enter into a close alliance with England, and maintain direct relations with her by means of a good commercial treaty; allow her even to exercise a certain monopoly in the interior of the State, so that a good understanding may be by degrees established between the English merchants and sailors and ours, who on their part are in favour of everything which tends to perfect and strengthen the Russian navy, by aid of which it is necessary to at once strive for mastery over the Baltic and in the Black Sea—the keystone on which the speedy success of the scheme depends.

VIII. Bear in mind that the commerce of India is the commerce of the world, and that he who can exclusively command it is dictator of Europe. No occasion should therefore be lost to provoke war with Persia, to hasten its decay, to advance on the Persian Gulf, and then to endeavour to re-establish the ancient trade of the Levant through Syria.

IX. Always interfere, either by force of arms or by intrigue, in the quarrels of the European Powers, and especially in those of Germany; and with this object:—

X. Seek after and maintain an alliance with Austria, encourage her in her favourite idea of national predominance, profit by the slightest ascendency gained over her to entangle her in disastrous wars, so that she may be gradually weakened; even help her sometimes; but incessantly stir up against her the enmity of the whole of Europe, but particularly of Germany, by rousing the jealousy and distrust of the German princes.

XI. Always select wives for Russian princes from among the German princesses, so that by thus multiplying alliances based on close relationship and mutual interest, we will increase our influence over that Empire.

XII. Make use of the power of the Church over the disunited and schismatical Greeks who are scattered over Hungary, Turkey, and the southern parts of Poland, gain them over by every possible means, pose as their protectors, and establish a claim to religious supremacy over them. Under this pretext, and with their help, Turkey will be conquered, and Poland, unable any longer to stand alone, either by its own strength or by means of political connections, will voluntarily place itself in subjection to us.

XIII. From that time every moment will be precious to us. All our batteries must be secretly prepared to strike the great blow, and so that they can strike with such order, precision, and rapidity as to give Europe no time for preparation. The first step will be to propose very secretly, and with the greatest circumspection, first to the Court of Versailles and then to that of Vienna, to divide with one of them the Empire of the World; and by mentioning that Russia is virtually ruler of the Eastern World, and has nothing to gain but the title, this proposal will probably not arouse their suspicion. It is undoubted that this project cannot fail to please them, and war will be kindled between them which will soon become general, both on account of the connections and widespread relationships between these two rival courts and natural enemies, and because of the interests which will compel the other Powers of Europe to take part in the struggle.

XIV. In the midst of this general discord, Russia will be asked for help, first by one and then by another of the belligerent powers; and having hesitated long enough to give them time to exhaust themselves, and to enable her to assemble her own armies, she will at last appear to decide in favour of the House of Austria, and while she pushes her irregular troops forward to the Rhine, she will at once follow them up with the hordes of Asia; and as they advance into Germany, two large fleets filled with a portion of the same hordes must set sail, one from the Sea of Azoff and the other from the port of Archangel, under convoy of war vessels from the Black Sea and Baltic. They will suddenly appear in the Mediterranean and Northern Ocean, and inundate Italy, Spain, and France with these fierce and rapacious nomads, who will plunder a portion of the inhabitants, carry off others into slavery to re-people the deserts of Siberia, and render the remainder incapable of escaping from our yoke. All these distractions will afford such great opportunities to the regular troops, that they will be able to act with a degree of energy and precision which will ensure the subjugation of the rest of Europe.

INDEX

THE END